We develop the vital bond of attachment via the smiling response.

As a visual stimulus the smile has attained its unique configuration principally by the simple act of turning up the mouth-corners. The mouth is opened to some extent and the lips pulled back, as in the face of fear, but by the addition of the curling up of the corners the character of the expression is radically changed. This development has in turn led to the possibility of another and contrasting facial posture—that of the down-turned mouth. By adopting a mouth-line that is the complete opposite of the smile shape, it is possible to signal an anti-smile. Just as laughing evolved out of crying and smiling out of laughing, so the unfriendly face has evolved, by a pendulum swing, from the friendly face.

But there is more to smiling than a mouth-line. As adults we may be able to convey our mood by a mere twist of the lips, but the infant throws much more into the battle. When smiling at full intensity, it also kicks and waves its arms about, stretches its hands out towards the stimulus and moves them about, produces babbling vocalisations, tilts back its head and protrudes its chin, leans its trunk forward or rolls it to one side, and exaggerates its respiration. Its eyes become brighter and may close slightly; wrinkles appear underneath or alongside the eyes and sometimes also on the bridge of the nose; the skin-fold between the sides of the nose and the sides of the mouth becomes more accentuated, and the tongue may be slightly protruded. Of these various elements the body movements seem to indicate a struggle on the infant's part to make contact with the mother. With its clumsy physique, the baby is probably showing us all that remains of the ancestral primate clinging response.

I have been dwelling on the baby's smile, but smiling is, of course, a two-way signal. When the infant smiles at its mother she responds with a similar signal. Each rewards the other and the bond between them tightens in both directions. You may feel that this is an obvious statement, but there can be a catch in it. Some mothers, when feeling agitated, anxious, or cross with the child, try to conceal their mood by forcing a smile. They hope that the counterfeit face will avoid upsetting the infant, but in reality this trick may do more harm than good. I mentioned earlier that it is almost impossible to fool a baby over questions of maternal mood. In the early years of life we seem to be acutely responsive to subtle signs of parental agitation and parental calm. At the pre-verbal stages, before the massive machinery of symbolic, cultural communication has bogged us down, we rely much more on tiny movements, postural changes and tones of voice than we need to in later life. Other species are particularly good at this, too. The astonishing ability of 'Clever Hans', the famous counting horse, was in fact based on its acuteness in responding to minute postural changes in his trainer. When asked to do a sum, Hans would tap his foot the appropriate number of times and then stop. Even if the trainer left the room and someone else took over, it still worked, because as the vital number of taps was reached, the stranger could not help tensing his body slightly. We all have this ability ourselves, even as adults (it is used a great deal by fortune-tellers to judge when they are on the right lines), but in pre-verbal infants it appears to be especially active. If the mother is making tense and agitated movements, no matter how concealed, she will communicate these to her child. If at the same time she gives a strong smile, it does not fool the infant, it only confuses it. Two conflicting messages are being transmitted. If this is done a great deal it may be permanently damaging and cause the child serious difficulties when making social contacts and adjustments later in life.

Leaving the subject of smiling, we must now turn to a very different activity. As the months pass, a new pattern of infant behaviour begins to emerge: aggression arrives on the scene. Temper tantrums and angry crying begin to differentiate themselves from the earlier all-purpose crying response. The baby signals its aggression by a more broken, irregular form of screaming and by violent striking out with its arms and legs. It attacks small objects, shakes large ones, spits and spews, and tries to bite, scratch or strike anything in reach. At first these activities are rather ran-

dom and unco-ordinated. The crying indicates that
fear is still present. The aggression has not yet matured
to the point of a pure attack: this will come much
later when the infant is sure of itself and fully aware
of its physical capacities. When it does develop, it, too,
has its own special facial signals. These consist of a
tight-lipped glare. The lips are pursed into a hard
line, with the mouth-corners held forward rather than
pulled back. The eyes stare fixedly at the opponent
and the eyebrows are lowered in a frown. The fists are
clenched. The child has begun to assert itself.

It has been found that this aggressiveness can be
increased by raising the density of a group of children. Under crowded conditions the friendly social
interactions between members of a group become
reduced, and the destructive and aggressive patterns
show a marked rise in frequency and intensity. This is
significant when one remembers that in other animals
fighting is used not only to sort out dominance disputes, but also to increase the spacing-out of the members of a species. We will return to this in Chapter
Five.

Apart from protecting, feeding, cleaning and playing with the offspring, the parental duties also include
the all-important process of training. As with other
species, this is done by a punishment-and-reward
system that gradually modifies and adjusts the trial-
and-error learning of the young. But, in addition, the
offspring will be learning rapidly by imitation—a process that is comparatively poorly developed in most
other mammals, but superbly heightened and refined
in ourselves. So much of what other animals must
laboriously learn for themselves, we acquire quickly
by following the example of our parents. The naked
ape is a teaching ape. (We are so attuned to this
method of learning that we tend to assume that other
species benefit in the same way, with the result that
we have grossly over-estimated the role that teaching
plays in their lives.)

Much of what we do as adults is based on this
imitative absorption during our childhood years. Frequently we imagine that we are behaving in a particular way because such behaviour accords with some

abstract, lofty code of moral principles, when in reality all we are doing is obeying a deeply ingrained and long 'forgotten' set of purely imitative impressions. It is the unmodifiable obedience to these impressions (along with our carefully concealed instinctive urges) that makes it so hard for societies to change their customs and their 'beliefs'. Even when faced with exciting, brilliantly rational new ideas, based on the application of pure, objective intelligence, the community will still cling to its old home-based habits and prejudices. This is the cross we have to bear if we are going to sail through our vital juvenile 'blotting-paper' phase of rapidly mopping up the accumulated experiences of previous generations. We are forced to take the biased opinions along with the valuable facts.

Luckily we have evolved a powerful antidote to this weakness which is inherent in the imitative learning process. We have a sharpened curiosity, an intensified urge to explore which work against the other tendency and produce a balance that has the potential of fantastic success. Only if a culture becomes too rigid as a result of its slavery to imitative repetition, or too daring and rashly exploratory, will it flounder. Those with a good balance between the two urges will thrive. We can see plenty of examples of the too rigid and too rash cultures around the world today. The small, backward societies, completely dominated by their heavy burden of taboos and ancient customs, are cases of the former. The same societies, when converted and 'aided' by advanced cultures, rapidly become examples of the latter. The sudden overdose of social novelty and exploratory excitement swamps the stabilising forces of ancestral imitation and tips the scales too far the other way. The result is cultural turmoil and disintegration. Lucky is the society that enjoys the gradual acquisition of a perfect balance between imitation and curiosity, between slavish, unthinking copying and progressive, rational experimentation.

CHAPTER FOUR

EXPLORATION

ALL mammals have a strong exploratory urge, but for some it is more crucial than others. It depends largely on how specialised they have become during the course of evolution. If they have put all their evolutionary effort into the perfection of one particular survival trick, they do not need to bother so much about the general complexities of the world around them. So long as the ant-eater has its ants and koala bear its gum leaves, then they are well satisfied and the living is easy. The non-specialists, on the other hand—the opportunists of the animal world—can never afford to relax. They are never sure where their next meal may be coming from, and they have to know every nook and cranny, test every possibility, and keep a sharp look-out for the lucky chance. They must explore, and keep on exploring. They must investigate, and keep on re-checking. They must have a constantly high level of curiosity.

It is not simply a matter of feeding: self-defence can make the same demands. Porcupines, hedgehogs and skunks can snuffle and stomp about as noisily as they like, heedless of their enemies, but the unarmed mammal must be forever on the alert. It must know the signs of danger and the routes of escape. To survive it must know its home range in every minute detail.

Looked at in this way, it might seem rather inefficient not to specialise. Why should there be any opportunist mammals at all? The answer is that there is a serious snag in the specialist way of life. Everything is fine as long as the special survival device works, but if the environment undergoes a major change the specialist is left stranded. If it has gone to sufficient extremes to outstrip its competitors, the animal will have been forced to make major changes in its genetical make-up, and it will not be able to reverse these quickly enough when the crunch comes. If the gum-tree forests were swept away the koala would perish. If an iron-mouthed killer developed the ability to munch up porcupine quills, the porcupine would become easy prey. For the opportunist the going may always be tough, but the creature will be able to adapt rapidly to any quick-change act that the environment decides to put on. Take away a mongoose's rats and mice and it will switch to eggs and snails. Take away a monkey's fruit and nuts and it will switch to roots and shoots.

Of all the non-specialists, the monkeys and apes are perhaps the most opportunist. As a group, they have specialised in non-specialisation. And among the monkeys and apes, the naked ape is the most supreme opportunist of them all. This is just another facet of his neotenous evolution. All young monkeys are inquisitive, but the intensity of their curiosity tends to fade as they become adult. With us, the infantile inquisitiveness is strengthened and stretched out into our mature years. We never stop investigating. We are never satisfied that we know enough to get by. Every question we answer leads on to another question. This has become the greatest survival trick of our species.

The tendency to be attracted by novelty has been called *neophilia* (love of the new), and has been contrasted with *neophobia* (fear of the new). Everything unfamiliar is potentially dangerous. It has to be approached with caution. Perhaps it should be avoided? But if it is avoided, then how shall we ever know anything about it? The neophilic urge must drive us on and keep us interested until the unknown has become the known, until familiarity has bred contempt and, in the process, we have gained valuable experience to be stored away and called upon when needed at a later date. The child does this all the time. So strong is his urge that parental restraint is necessary. But although parents may succeed in guiding curiosity, they can never suppress it. As children grow older their exploratory tendencies sometimes reach alarming proportions and adults can be heard referring to 'a group of youngsters behaving like wild animals'.

But the reverse is actually the case. If the adults took the trouble to study the way in which adult wild animals really do behave, they would find that *they* are the wild animals. They are the ones who are trying to limit exploration and who are selling out to the cosiness of sub-human conservativism. Luckily for the species, there are always enough adults who retain their juvenile inventiveness and curiosity and who enable populations to progress and expand.

When we look at young chimpanzees at play we are immediately struck by the similarity between their behaviour and that of our own children. Both are fascinated by new 'toys'. They fall on them eagerly, lifting them, dropping them, twisting them, banging them and taking them to pieces. They both invent simple games. The intensity of their interest is as strong as ours, and during the first few years of life they do just as well—better, in fact, because their muscle system develops quicker. But after a while they begin to lose ground. Their brains are not complex enough to build on this good beginning. Their powers of concentration are weak and do not grow as their bodies grow. Above all, they lack the ability to communicate in detail with their parents about the inventive techniques they are discovering.

The best way to clarify this difference is to take a specific example. Picture-making, or graphic exploration, is an obvious choice. As a pattern of behaviour it has been vitally important to our species for thousands of years, and we have the prehistoric remnants at Altamira and Lascaux to prove it.

Given the opportunity and suitable materials, young chimpanzees are as excited as we are to explore the visual possibilities of making marks on a blank sheet of paper. The start of this interest has something to do with the investigation-reward principle of obtaining disproportionately large results from the expenditure of comparatively little energy. This can be seen operating in all kinds of play situations. A great deal of exaggerated effort may be put into the activities, but it is those actions that produce an unexpectedly increased feed-back that are the most satisfying. We can call this the play principle of 'magnified reward'.

Both chimps and children like banging things and it is those objects which produce the loudest noise for the smallest effort that are preferred. Balls that bounce high when only weakly thrown, balloons that shoot across a room when only lightly touched, sand that can be moulded with the mildest pressure, toys on wheels that roll easily along at the gentlest push, these are the things that have maximum play-appeal.

When first faced with a pencil and paper the infant does not find itself in a very promising situation. The best it can do is to tap the pencil on to the surface. But this leads to a pleasant surprise. The tap does something more than simply make a noise, it produces a visual impact as well. Something comes out of the end of the pencil and leaves a mark on the paper. A line is drawn.

It is fascinating to watch this first moment of graphic discovery by a chimpanzee or a child. It stares at the line, intrigued by the unexpected visual bonus its action has brought. After viewing the result for a moment it repeats the experiment. Sure enough, it works the second time, then again, and again. Soon the sheet is covered with scribble lines. As time passes, drawing sessions become more vigorous. Single, tentative lines, placed on the paper one after the other, give way to multiple back-and-forth scribbling. If there is a choice, crayons, chalks and paints are preferred to pencils because they have an even bolder impact, produce an even bigger visual effect, as they sweep across the paper.

The first interest in this activity appears at about one-and-a-half years of age, in both chimps and children. But it is not until after the second birthday that the bold, confident, multiple scribbling really gains momentum. At the age of three the average child moves into a new graphic phase: it starts to simplify its confused scribbling. Out of the exciting chaos it begins to distil basic shapes. It experiments with crosses, then with circles, squares and triangles. Meandering lines are led round the page until they join up with themselves, enclosing a space. A line becomes an outline.

During the months that follow, these simple shapes

are combined, one with another, to produce simple abstract patterns. A circle is cut through by a cross, the corners of a square are joined by diagonal lines. This is the vital stage that precedes the very first pictorial representations. In the child this great breakthrough comes in the second half of the third year, or the beginning of the fourth. In the chimpanzee, it never comes. The young chimp manages to make fanpatterns, crosses and circles, and it can even achieve a 'marked circle', but it can go no further. It is particularly tantalising that the marked-circle motif is the immediate precursor of the earliest representation produced by the typical child. What happens is that a few lines or spots are placed inside the outline of the circle and then, as if by magic, a face stares back at the infant painter. There is a sudden flash of recognition. The phase of abstract experimentation, of pattern invention, is over. Now a new goal must be reached: the goal of perfected representation. New faces are made, better faces, with the eyes and mouth in the right place. Details are added—hair, ears, a nose, arms and legs. Other images are born—flowers, houses, animals, boats, cars. These are heights the young chimp can never, it seems, attain. After the peak has been reached—the circle made and its inside area marked—the animal continues to grow but its pictures do not. Perhaps one day a genius chimp will be found, but it seems unlikely.

For the child, the representational phase of graphic exploration now stretches out before it, but although it is the major area of discovery, the older abstract patterning influences still make themselves felt, especially between the ages of five and eight. During this period particularly attractive paintings are produced because they are based on the solid grounding of the abstract-shape phase. The representational images are still at a very simple stage of differentiation and they combine appealingly with the confident, well-established shape-and-pattern arrangements.

The process by which the dot-filled circle grows into an accurate full-length portrait is an intriguing one. The discovery that it represents a face does not lead to an overnight success in perfecting the process. This clearly becomes the dominant aim, but it takes time (more than a decade, in fact). To start with, the basic features have to be tidied up a little—circles for eyes, a good strong horizontal line for a mouth, two dots or a central circle for a nose. Hairs have to fringe the outer circle. And there things can pause for a while. The face, after all, is the most visual and compelling part of the mother, at least in visual terms. After a while, though, further progress is made. By the simple device of making some of the hairs longer than the rest, it is possible for this face-figure to sprout arms and legs. These in turn can grow fingers and toes. At this point the basic figure-shape is still founded on the pre-representational circle. This is an old friend and he is staying late. Having become a face he has now become a face and body combined. It does not seem to worry the child at this stage that the arms of its drawing are coming out of the side of what appears to be its head. But the circle cannot hold out for ever. Like a cell, it must divide and bud off a lower, second cell. Alternatively the two legs must be joined somewhere along their length, but higher than the feet. In one of these two ways, a body can be born. Whichever happens, it leaves the arms high and dry, sticking out of the side of the head. And there they stay for quite some time, before they are brought down into their more correct position, protruding from the top of the body.

It is fascinating to observe these slow steps being taken, one after the other, as the voyage of discovery tirelessly continues. Gradually more and more shapes and combinations are attempted, more diverse images, more complex colours, and more varied textures. Eventually, accurate representation is achieved and precise copies of the outside world can be trapped and preserved on paper. But at that stage the original exploratory nature of the activity becomes submerged beneath the pressing demands of pictorial communication. Earlier painting and drawing, in the young chimp and the young child, had nothing to do with the act of communicating. It was an act of discovery, of invention, of testing the possibilities of graphic variability. It was 'action-painting', not signalling. It required no reward—it was its own reward, it was play for play's sake. However, like so many aspects of childhood play, it soon becomes merged into other adult pursuits. Social communication makes a take-over bid for it and the original inventiveness is lost, the pure thrill of 'taking a line for a walk' is gone. Only in doodles do most adults allow it to re-emerge. (This does not mean that they have become uninventive, merely that the area of invention has moved on into more complex, technological spheres.)

Fortunately for the exploratory art of painting and drawing, much more efficient technical methods of reproducing images of the environment have now been developed. Photography and its offshoots have rendered representational 'information painting' obsolete. This has broken the heavy chains of responsibility that have been the crippling burden of adult art for so long. Painting can now once again explore, this time in a mature adult form. And this, one need hardly mention, is precisely what it is doing today.

I selected this particular example of exploratory behaviour because it reveals very clearly the differences between us and our nearest living relative, the chimpanzee. Similar comparisons could be made in other spheres. One or two deserve brief mention. Exploration of the world of sound can be observed in both species. Vocal invention, as we have already seen, is for some reason virtually absent in the chimpanzee, but 'percussive drumming' plays an important role in its life. Young chimpanzees repeatedly investigate the noise-potentials of acts of thumping, foot-stamping and clapping. As adults they develop this tendency into prolonged social drumming sessions. One animal after another stamps, screams and tears up vegetation, beating on tree-stumps and hollow logs. These communal displays may last for half an hour or more. Their exact function is unknown, but they have the effect of mutually arousing the members of a group. In our own species, drumming is also the most widespread form of musical expression. It begins early, as in the chimpanzee, when children begin to test out the percussive values of objects around them in much the same way. But whereas the adult chimpanzees never manage much more than a simple rhythmic tattoo, we elaborate it into complex poly-rhythms and augment it with vibrating rattles and pitch variations. We also make additional noises by blowing into hollow cavities and scraping or plucking pieces of metal. The screams and hoots of the chimpanzee become in us inventive chants. Our development of complicated musical performances appears, in simpler social groups, to have played much the same role as the drumming and hooting sessions of the chimpanzees, namely, mutual group arousal. Unlike picture-making, it was not an activity pattern that became commandeered for the transmission of detailed information on a major scale. The sending of messages by drumming sequences in certain cultures was an exception to this rule, but by and large music was developed as a communal mood-provoker and synchroniser. Its inventive and exploratory content became stronger and stronger, however, and, freed of any important 'representational' duties, it has become a major area of abstract aesthetic experimentation. (Because of its other prior information commitments, painting has only just caught up with it.)

Dancing has followed much the same course as music and singing. The chimpanzees include many swaying and jigging movements in their drumming rituals and these also accompany the mood-provoking musical performances of our own species. From there, like music, they have been elaborated and expanded into aesthetically complex performances.

Closely related to dancing has been the growth of gymnastics. Rhythmical physical performances are common in the play of both young chimps and young children. They rapidly become stylised, but retain a strong element of variability within the structured patterns they assume. But the physical games of chimpanzees do not grow and mature, they fizzle out. We, on the other hand, explore their possibilities to the full and elaborate them in our adult lives into many complex forms of exercises and sports. Again they are important as communal synchronising devices, but essentially they are means of maintaining and expanding our exploration of our physical capacities.

Writing, a formalised offshoot of picture-making, and verbalised vocal communication have, of course, been developed as our major means of transmitting and recording information, but they have also been utilised as vehicles for aesthetic exploration on an enormous scale. The intricate elaboration of our ancestral grunts and squeaks into complex symbolic speech has enabled us to sit and 'play' with thoughts in our heads, and to manipulate our (primarily instructional) word sequences to new ends as aesthetic, experimental play-things.

So, in all these spheres—in painting, sculpture, drawing, music, singing, dancing, gymnastics, games, sports, writing and speech—we can carry on to our heart's content, all through our long lives, complex and specialised forms of exploration and experiment. Through elaborate training, both as performers and observers, we can sensitise our responsiveness to the immense exploratory potential that these pursuits have to offer. If we set aside the secondary functions of these activities (the making of money, gaining of status, and so forth), then they all emerge, biologically, either as the extension into adult life of infantile play-patterns, or as the superimposition on to adult information-communication systems of 'play-rules'.

These rules can be stated as follows: (1) you shall investigate the unfamiliar until it has become familiar; (2) you shall impose rhythmic repetition on the familiar; (3) you shall vary this repetition in as many ways as possible; (4) you shall select the most satisfying of these variations and develop these at the expense of others; (5) you shall combine and recombine these variations one with another; and (6) you shall do all this for its own sake, as an end in itself.

These principles apply from one end of the scale to the other, whether you are considering an infant playing in the sand, or a composer working on a symphony.

The last rule is particularly important. Exploratory behaviour also plays a role in the basic survival patterns of feeding, fighting, mating and the rest. But there it is confined to the early appetitive phases of the activity sequences and is geared to their special demands. For many species of animals it is no more than this. There is no exploration for exploration's sake. But, amongst the higher mammals and to a supreme extent in ourselves, it has become emancipated as a distinct, separate drive. Its function is to provide us with as subtle and complex an awareness of the world around us, and of our own capacities in relation to it, as possible. This awareness is not heightened in the specific contexts of the basic survival goals, but in generalised terms. What we acquire in this way can then be applied anywhere, at any time, in any context.

I have omitted the growth of science and technology from this discussion because it has largely been concerned with specific improvements in the methods employed in achieving the basic survival goals, such as fighting (weapons), feeding (agriculture), nest building (architecture) and comfort (medicine). It is interesting, though, that as time has gone by and the technical developments have become more and more interlocked with one another, the pure exploratory urge has also invaded the scientific sphere. Scientific research—the very name 're-search' gives the game away (and I mean game)—operates very much on the play-principles mentioned earlier. In 'pure' research, the scientist uses his imagination in virtually the same way as the artist. He talks of a beautiful experiment rather than of an expedient one. Like the artist, he is concerned with exploration for exploration's sake. If the results of the studies prove to be useful in the context of some specific survival goal, all to the good, but this is secondary.

In all exploratory behaviour, whether artistic or scientific, there is the ever-present battle between the neophilic and neophobic urges. The former drives us on to new experiences, makes us crave for novelty. The latter holds us back, makes us take refuge in the familiar. We are constantly in a state of shifting balance between the conflicting attractions of the exciting new stimulus and the friendly old one. If we lost our neophilia we would stagnate. If we lost our neophobia, we would rush headlong into disaster. This state of conflict does not merely account for the more obvious fluctuations in fashions and fads, in hair-styles and clothing, in furniture and cars; it is also the very basis of our whole cultural progression. We explore and we retrench, we investigate and we stabilise. Step by step we expand our awareness and understanding both of ourselves and of the complex environment we live in.

Before leaving this topic there is one final, special aspect of exploratory behaviour that cannot go unmentioned. It concerns a critical phase of social play during the infantile period. When it is very young, the infant's social play is directed primarily at the parents, but as it grows the emphasis is shifted from them towards other children of the same age. The child becomes a member of a juvenile 'play group'. This is a critical step in its development. As an exploratory involvement it has far-reaching effects on the later life of the individual. Of course, all forms of exploration at this tender age have long-term consequences—the child that fails to explore music or painting will find these subjects difficult as an adult—but person-to-person play contacts are even more critical than the rest. An adult coming to music, say, for the first time, without childhood exploration of the subject behind him, may find it difficult, but not impossible. A child that has been severely sheltered from social contact as a member of a play group, on the other hand, will always find himself badly hampered in his adult social interactions. Experiments with monkeys have revealed that not only does isolation in infancy produce a socially withdrawn adult, but it also creates an anti-sexual and anti-parental individual. Monkeys that were reared in isolation from other youngsters failed to participate in play-group activities when exposed to them later, as older juveniles. Although the isolates were physically healthy and had grown well in their solitary states, they were quite incapable of joining in the general rough and tumble. Instead they crouched, immobile, in the corner of the play-room, usually clasping their bodies tightly with their arms, or covering their eyes. When they matured, again as physically healthy specimens, they showed no interest in sexual partners. If forcibly mated, female isolates produced offspring in the normal way, but then proceeded to treat them as though they were huge parasites crawling on their bodies. They attacked them, drove them away, and either killed them or ignored them.

Similar experiments with young chimpanzees showed that, in this species, with prolonged rehabilitation and special care it was possible to undo, to some extent, this behavioural damage, but, even so, over-protected children will always suffer in adult social contacts. This is especially important in the case of only children, where the absence of siblings sets them at a serious initial disadvantage. If they do not experience the socialising effects of the rough-and-tumble of the juvenile play groups, they are liable to remain shy and withdrawn for the rest of their lives, find sexual pair-bonding difficult or impossible and, if they do manage to become parents, will make bad ones.

From this it is clear that the rearing process has two distinct phases—an early, inward-turning one and a later, outward-turning one. They are both vitally important and we can learn a great deal about them from monkey behaviour. During the early phase the infant is loved, rewarded and protected by the mother. It comes to understand security. In the later phase it is encouraged to be more outward-going, to participate in social contacts with other juveniles. The mother becomes less loving and restricts her protective acts to moments of serious panic or alarm, when outside dangers threaten the colony. She may now actually punish the growing offspring if it persists in clinging to her hairy apron-strings in the absence of serious panic. It now comes to understand and accept its growing independence.

The situation should be basically the same for offspring of our own species. If either of these basic phases is parentally mis-handled, the child will be in serious trouble in later life. If it has lacked the early security phase, but has been suitably active in the independence phase, it will find making new social contacts easy enough, but will be unable to maintain them or make any real depth of contact. If it has enjoyed great security in the early phase, but has been over-protected later on, it will find making new adult contacts immensely difficult and will tend to cling desperately to old ones.

If we take a closer look at the more extreme cases of social withdrawal, we can witness anti-exploratory behaviour in its most extreme and characteristic form. Severely withdrawn individuals may become socially inactive, but they are far from physically inactive. They become preoccupied with repetitive stereotypes. For hour after hour they rock or sway, nod or shake, twirl or twitch, or clasp and unclasp themselves. They may suck their thumbs, or other parts of their bodies, prod or pinch themselves, make strange and repetitive facial expressions, or tap or roll small objects rhythmically. We all exhibit 'tics' of this sort occasionally, but for them it becomes a major and prolonged form of physical expression. What happens is that they find the environment so threatening, social contacts so frightening and impossible, that they seek comfort and reassurance by super-familiarising their behaviour. The rhythmic repetition of an act renders it increasingly familiar and 'safe'. Instead of performing a wide variety of heterogeneous activities, the withdrawn individual sticks to the few he knows best. For him the old saying: 'Nothing ventured, nothing gained' has been re-written: 'Nothing ventured, nothing lost.'

I have already mentioned the comforting regressive qualities of the heart-beat rhythm, and this applies here, too. Many of the patterns seem to operate at about heart-beat speed, but even those that do not, still act as 'comforters' by virtue of their super-familiarity achieved from constant repetition. It has been noticed that socially retarded individuals increase their stereotypes when put into a strange room. This fits in with the ideas expressed here. The increased novelty of the environment heightens the neophobic fears, and heavier demands are made on the comforting devices to counteract this.

The more a stereotype is repeated, the more it becomes like an artificially produced, maternal heart-beat. Its 'friendliness' increases and increases until it becomes virtually irreversible. Even if the extreme neophobia causing it can be removed (which is difficult enough), the stereotype may go twitching on.

As I said, socially adjusted individuals also exhibit these 'tics' from time to time. Usually they occur in stress situations and here, too, they act as comforters. We know all the signs. The executive awaiting a vital phone call taps or drums on his desk; the woman in the doctor's waiting-room, clasps and unclasps her fingers around her handbag; the embarrassed child swings its body left and right, left and right; the expectant father paces back and forth; the student in the exam sucks his pencil; the anxious officer strokes his moustache. In moderation these little anti-exploratory devices are useful. They help us to tolerate the anticipated 'novelty overdose'. If used to excess, however, there is always the danger that they will become irreversible and obsessive, and will persist even when not called for.

Stereotypes also crop up in situations of extreme boredom. This can be seen very clearly in zoo animals as well as in our own species. It can sometimes reach frightening proportions. What happens here is that the captive animals would make social contacts if only they had the chance, but they are physically prevented from doing so. The situation is basically the same as in cases of social withdrawal. The restricted environment of the zoo cage blocks their social contacts and forces them into a situation of social withdrawal. The cage-bars are a solid, physical equivalent of the psychological barriers facing the socially withdrawn individual. They constitute a powerful anti-exploratory device and, left with nothing to explore, the zoo animal begins to express itself in the only way possible, by developing rhythmic stereotypes. We are all familiar with the repetitive pacing to-and-fro of the caged animal, but this is only one of the many strange patterns that arise. Stylised masturbation may occur. Sometimes this no longer involves manipulation of the penis. The animal (usually a monkey) simply makes the back and forth masturbatory movements of its arm and hand, but without actually touching the penis. Some female monkeys repeatedly suck their own nipples. Young animals suck their paws. Chimpanzees may prod pieces of straw into their (previous healthy) ears. Elephants nod their heads for hours on end. Certain creatures repeatedly bite themselves, or pull their own hair out. Serious self-mutilation may occur. Some of these responses are given in stressful situations, but many of them are simply reactions to boredom. When there is no variability in the environment the exploratory urge stagnates.

Simply by looking at an isolated animal performing one of these stereotypes it is impossible to know for certain what is causing the behaviour. It may be boredom, or it may be stress. If it is stress it may be the result of the immediate environmental situation, or it may be a long-term phenomenon stemming from an abnormal upbringing. A few simple experiments can give us the answer. When a strange object is placed in the cage, if the stereotypes disappear and exploration begins, then they were obviously being caused by boredom. If the stereotypes increase, however, then they were being caused by stress. If they persist after the introduction of other members of the same species, producing a normal social environment, then the individual with the stereotypes has almost certainly had an abnormally isolated infancy.

All these zoo peculiarities can be seen in our own species (perhaps because we have designed our zoos so much like our cities). They should be a lesson to us, reminding us of the enormous importance of achieving a good balance between our neophobic and neophilic tendencies. If we do not have this, we cannot function properly. Our nervous systems will do the best they can for us, but the results will always be a travesty of our true behavioural potentials.

CHAPTER FIVE

FIGHTING

IF we are to understand the nature of our aggressive urges, we must see them against the background of our animal origins. As a species we are so preoccupied with mass-produced and mass-destroying violence at the present time, that we are apt to lose our objectivity when discussing this subject. It is a fact that the most level-headed intellectuals frequently become violently aggressive when discussing the urgent need to suppress aggression. This is not surprising. We are, to put it mildly, in a mess, and there is a strong chance that we shall have exterminated ourselves by the end of the century. Our only consolation will have to be that, as a species, we have had an exciting term of office. Not a long term, as species go, but an amazingly eventful one. But before we examine our own bizarre perfections of attack and defence, we must examine the basic nature of violence in the spearless, gunless, bombless world of animals.

Animals fight amongst themselves for one of two very good reasons: either to establish their dominance in a social hierarchy, or to establish their territorial rights over a particular piece of ground. Some species are purely hierarchical, with no fixed territories. Some are purely territorial, with no hierarchy problems. Some have hierarchies on their territories and have to contend with both forms of aggression. We belong to the last group: we have it both ways. As primates we were already loaded with the hierarchy system. This is the basic way of primate life. The group keeps moving about, rarely staying anywhere long enough to establish a fixed territory. Occasional inter-group conflict may arise, but it is weakly organised, spasmodic and of comparatively little importance in the life of the average monkey. The 'peck order' (so-called because it was first discussed in respect of chickens) is, on the other hand, of vital significance in his day-to-day—and even his minute-to-minute—living. There is a rigidly established social hierarchy in most species of monkeys and apes, with a dominant male in charge of the group, and the others ranged below him in varying degrees of subordination. When he becomes too old or weak to maintain his domination, he is overthrown by a younger, sturdier male, who then assumes the mantle of the colony boss. (In some cases the usurper literally assumes the mantle, growing one in the form of a cape of long hair.) As the troop keeps together all the time, his role as group tyrant is incessantly operative. But despite this he is invariably the sleekest, best-groomed and sexiest monkey in the community.

Not all primate species are violently dictatorial in their social organisation. There is nearly always a tyrant, but he is sometimes a benign and rather tolerant tyrant, as in the case of the mighty gorilla. He shares the females amongst the lesser males, is generous at feeding times, and only asserts himself when something crops up that cannot be shared, or when there are signs of a revolt, or unruly fighting amongst the weaker members.

This basic system obviously had to be changed when the naked ape became a co-operative hunter with a fixed home base. Just as with sexual behaviour, the typical primate system had to be modified to match his adopted carnivore role. The group had to become territorial. It had to defend the region of its fixed base. Because of the co-operative nature of the hunting, this had to be done on a group basis, rather than individually. Within the group the tyrannical hierarchy system of the usual primate colony had to be modified considerably to ensure full co-operation from the weaker members when out hunting. But it could not be abolished altogether. There had to be a mild hierarchy, with stronger members and a top leader, if firm decisions were going to be taken, even if this leader was obliged to take the feelings of his inferiors more into account than his hairy, forest-dwelling equivalent would have to do.

In addition to group defence of territory and hierarchy organisation, the prolonged dependency of the young, forcing us to adopt pair-bonded family units, demanded yet another form of self-assertion. Each male, as the head of a family, became involved in defending his own individual home base inside the general colony base. So for us there are three fundamental forms of aggression, instead of the usual one or two. As we know to our cost, they are all still very much in evidence today, despite the complexities of our societies.

How does the aggression work? What are the patterns of behaviour involved? How do we intimidate one another? We must look again at the other animals. When a mammal becomes aggressively aroused a number of basic physiological changes occur within its body. The whole machine has to gear itself up for action, by means of the autonomic nervous system. This system consists of two opposing and counterbalancing sub-systems—the sympathetic and the parasympathetic. The former is the one that is concerned with preparing the body for violent activity. The latter has the task of preserving and restoring bodily reserves. The former says, 'You are stripped for action, get moving;' the latters says, 'Take it easy, relax and conserve your strength.' Under normal circumstances the body listens to both these voices and maintains a happy balance between them, but when strong aggression is aroused it listens only to the sympathetic system. When this is activated, adrenalin pours into the blood and the whole circulatory system is profoundly affected. The hearts beats faster and blood is transferred from the skin and viscera to the muscles and brain. There is an increase in blood pressure. The rate of production of red blood corpuscles is rapidly stepped up. There is a reduction of the time taken for blood to coagulate. In addition there is a cessation in the processes of digesting and storing food. Salivation is restrained. Movements of the stomach, the secretion of gastric juices, and the peristaltic movements of the intestines are all inhibited. Also, the rectum and bladder do not empty as easily as under normal conditions. Stored carbohydrate is rushed out of the liver and floods the blood with sugar. There is a massive increase in respiratory activity. Breathing becomes quicker and deeper. The temperature-regulating mechanisms are activated. The hair stands on end and there is profuse sweating.

All these changes assist in preparing the animal for battle. As if by magic, they instantly banish fatigue and make large amounts of energy available for the anticipated physical struggle for survival. The blood is pumped vigorously to the sites where it is most needed —to the brain, for quick thinking, and to the muscles, for violent action. The rise in blood sugars increases muscular efficiency. The speeding up of coagulation processes means that any blood spilled as a result of injury will clot more quickly and reduce wastage. The stepped-up release of red blood cells from the spleen, in combination with the increased speed of blood circulation, aids the respiratory system to boost the intake of oxygen and the removal of carbon dioxide. The full hair erection exposes the skin to the air and helps to cool the body, as does the outpouring of sweat from the sweat glands. The dangers of over-heating from excessive activity are therefore reduced.

With all the vital systems activated, the animal is ready to launch into the attack, but there is a snag. Out-and-out fighting may lead to a valuable victory, but it may also involve serious damage to the victor. The enemy invariably provokes fear as well as aggression. The aggression drives the animal on, the fear holds it back. An intense state of inner conflict arises. Typically, the animal that is aroused to fight does not go straight into an all-out attack. It begins by threatening to attack. Its inner conflict suspends it, tensed for combat, but not yet ready to begin it. If, in this state, it presents a sufficiently intimidating spectacle for its opponent, and the latter slinks away, then obviously this is preferable. The victory can be won without the shedding of blood. The species is able to settle its disputes without undue damage to its members and obviously benefits tremendously in the process.

Throughout the higher forms of animal life there has been a strong trend in this direction—the direction of ritualised combat. Threat and counter-threat has largely replaced actual physical combat. Full-blooded fighting does, of course, still take place from time to time, but only as a last resort, when aggressive signalling and counter-signalling have failed to settle a dispute. The strength of the outward signs of the physiological changes I have described indicates to the enemy just how violently the aggressive animal is preparing itself for action.

This works extremely well behaviourally, but physiologically it creates something of a problem. The machinery of the body has been geared up for a massive output of work. But the anticipated exertions do not materialise. How does the autonomic nervous system deal with this situation? It has mustered all its troops at the front line, ready for action, but their very presence has won the war. What happens now?

If physical combat followed on naturally from the massive activation of the sympathetic nervous system, all the body preparations it had made would be fully utilised. The energy would be burned up and eventually the parasympathetic system would reassert itself and gradually restore a state of physiological calm. But in the tense state of conflict between aggression and fear, everything is suspended. The result is that the parasympathetic system fights back wildly and the autonomic pendulum swings frantically back and forth. As the tense moments of threat and counter-threat tick by, we see flashes of parasympathetic activity interspersed with the sympathetic symptoms. Dryness in the mouth may give way to excessive salivation. Tightening of the bowels may collapse and sudden defecation may occur. The urine, held back so strongly in the bladder, may be released in a flood. The removal of blood from the skin may be massively reversed, extreme pallor being replaced by intense flushing and reddening. The deep and rapid respiration may be dramatically interrupted, leading to gasps and sighs. These are desperate attempts on the part of the parasympathetic system to counteract the apparent extravagance of the sympathetic. Under normal circumstances it would be out of the question for intense reactions in one direction to occur simultaneously with intense reactions in the other, but under the extreme conditions of aggressive threat, everything gets momentarily out of phase. (This explains why, in extreme cases of shock, fainting or swooning can be observed. In such instances the blood that has been rushed to the brain is withdrawn again so violently that it leads to sudden unconsciousness.)

As far as the threat signalling-system is concerned, this physiological turbulence is a gift. It provides an even richer source of signals. During the course of evolution these mood-signs have been built on and elaborated in a number of ways. Defecation and urination have become important territorial scent-marking devices for many species of mammals. The most commonly seen example of this is the way domestic dogs cock their legs against marker-posts in their territories, and the way this activity is increased during threatening encounters between rival dogs. (The streets of our cities are excessively stimulating for this activity because they constitute overlapping territories for so many rivals, and each dog is forced to super-scent these areas in an attempt to compete.) Some species have evolved super-dunging techniques. The hippopotamus has acquired a specially flattened tail that is waggled rapidly back and forth during the act of defecating. The effect is that of shooting dung through a fan, with the result that the faeces are spread out over a wide area. Many species have developed special anal glands that add strong personal scents to the dung.

The circulatory disturbances producing extreme pallor or intense red flushes have become improved as signals by the development of bare patches of skin on the faces of many species and the rumps of others. The gaping and hissing of the respiratory disturbances have been elaborated into grunts and roars and the many other aggressive vocalisations. It has been suggested that this accounts for the origin of the whole communication system of vocal signals. Another basic trend developing out of respiratory turbulence is the evolution of inflation displays. Many species puff themselves up in threat and may inflate specialised air-sacs and pouches. (This is particularly common amongst birds, which already possess a number of air-sacs as a basic part of their respiratory systems.)

Aggressive hair-erection has led to the growth of specialised regions such as crests, capes, manes and fringes. These and other localised hair patches have become highly conspicuous. The hairs have become elongated or stiffened. Their pigmentation has often been drastically modified to produce areas of strong contrast with the surrounding fur. When aggressively aroused, with the hairs standing on end, the animal suddenly appears larger and more frightening, and the display patches become bigger and brighter.

Aggressive sweating has become another source of scent-signals. In many cases there have, once again, been specialised evolutionary trends exploiting this possibility. Certain of the sweat glands have become enormously enlarged as complex scent-glands. These can be found on the faces, feet, tails and various parts of the body of many species.

All these improvements have enriched the communication systems of animals and rendered their mood language more subtle and informative. They make the threatening behaviour of the aroused animal more 'readable' in more precise terms.

But this is only half the story. We have been considering only the autonomic signals. In addition to all these there is another whole range of signals available, which stem from the tensed-up muscular movements and postures of the threatening animal. All that the autonomic system did was to gear the body up ready for muscular action. But what did the muscles do about it? They were stiffened for the onslaught, but no onslaught came. The outcome of this situation is a series of aggressive intention movements, ambivalent actions, and conflict postures. The impulses to attack and to flee pull the body this way and that. It lunges forward, pulls back, twists sideways, crouches down, leaps up, leans in, tilts away. As soon as the urge to attack gets the upper hand, the impulse to flee immediately countermands the order. Every move to withdraw is checked by a move to attack. During the course of evolution this general agitation has become modified into specialised postures of threat and intimidation. The intention movements have become stylised, the ambivalent jerkings have become formalised into rhythmic twistings and shakings. A whole new repertoire of aggressive signals has been developed and perfected.

As a result of this we can witness, in many animal species, elaborate threat rituals and combat 'dances'. The contestants circle one another in a characteristically stilted fashion, their bodies tense and stiff. They may bow, nod, shake, shiver, swing rhythmically from side to side, or make repeated short, stylised runs. They paw the ground, arch their backs, or lower their heads. All these intention movements act as vital communication signals and combine effectively with the autonomic signals to provide a precise picture of the intensity of the aggression that has been aroused, and an exact indication of the balance between the urge to attack and the urge to flee.

But there is yet more to come. There is another important source of special signals, arising from a category of behaviour that has been named displacement activity. One of the side-effects of an intense inner conflict is that an animal sometimes exhibits strange and seemingly irrelevant pieces of behaviour. It is as if the tensed-up creature, unable to perform either of the things it is desperate to do, finds an outlet for its pent-up energy in some other, totally unrelated activity. Its urge to flee blocks its urge to attack and vice-versa, so it vents its feelings in some other way. Threatening rivals can be seen suddenly to perform curiously stilted and incomplete feeding movements, and then return instantly to their full threat postures. Or they may scratch or clean themselves in some way, interspersing these movements with the typical threat manoeuvring. Some species perform displacement nest-building actions, picking up pieces of nest material that happen to lie near by and dropping them on to imaginary nests. Others indulge in 'instant sleep', momentarily tucking their heads into a snoozing position, yawning or stretching.

There has been a great deal of controversy about these displacement activities. It has been argued that there is no objective justification for referring to them as irrelevancies. If an animal feeds, it is hungry, and if it scratches it must itch. It is stressed that it is impossible to prove that a threatening animal is not hungry when it performs so-called displacement feeding actions, or that it is not itching when it scratches. But this is armchair criticism, and to anyone who has actually observed and studied aggressive encounters in a wide variety of species, it is patently absurd. The tension and drama of these moments is such that it is ridiculous to suggest that the contestants would break off, even momentarily, to feed for the sake of feeding, or scratch for the sake of scratching, or sleep for the sake of sleeping.

Despite the academic arguments about the causal mechanisms involved in the production of displacement activities, one thing is clear, namely that in functional terms they provide yet one more source for the evolution of valuable threat signals. Many animals have exaggerated these actions in such a way that they have become increasingly conspicuous and showy.

All these activities, then, the autonomic signals, the intention movements, the ambivalent postures and the displacement activities, become ritualised and together provide the animals with a comprehensive repertoire of threat signals. In most encounters they will be sufficient to resolve the dispute without the contestants coming to blows. But if this system fails, as it often does under conditions of extreme crowding, for example, then real fighting follows and the signals give way to the brutal mechanics of physical attack. Then, the teeth are used to bite, slash and stab, the head and horns to butt and spear, the body to ram, bump and push, the legs to claw, kick and swipe, the hands to grasp and squeeze, and sometimes the tail to thrash and whip. Even so, it is extremely rare for one contestant to kill the other. Species that have evolved special killing techniques for dealing with their prey seldom employ these when fighting their own kind. (Serious errors have sometimes been made in this connection, with false assumptions about the presumed relationship between prey-attacking behaviour and rival-attacking activities. The two are quite distinct in both motivation and performance.) As soon as the enemy has been sufficiently subdued, it ceases to be a threat and is ignored. There is no point in wasting additional energy on it, and it is allowed to slink away without further damage or persecution.

Before relating all these belligerent activities to our own species, there is one more aspect of animal aggression that must be examined. It concerns the behaviour of the loser. When his position has become untenable, the obvious thing for him to do is to remove himself as fast as he can. But this is not always possible. His escape route may be physically obstructed, or, if he is a member of a tightly knit social group, he may be obliged to stay within range of the victor. In either of these cases, he must somehow signal to the stronger animal that he is no longer a threat and that he does not intend to continue the fight. If he leaves it until he is badly damaged or physically exhausted, this will become obvious enough, and the dominant animal will wander off and leave him in peace. But if can signal his acceptance of defeat before his position has deteriorated to this unfortunate extreme, he will be able to avoid further serious punishment. This is achieved by the performance of certain characteristic submissive displays. These appease the attacker and rapidly reduce his aggression, speeding up the settlement of the dispute.

They operate in several ways. Basically, they either switch off the signals that have been arousing the aggression, or they switch on other, positively non-aggressive signals. The first category simply serve to calm the dominant animal down, the latter help by actively changing his mood into something else. The crudest form of submission is gross inactivity. Because aggression involves violent movement, a static pose automatically signals non-aggression. Frequently this is combined with crouching and cowering. Aggression involves expanding the body to its maximum size, and crouching reverses this and therefore acts as an appeasement. Facing away from the attacker also helps, being the opposite of the posture of frontal attack. Other threat-opposites are also used. If a particular species threatens by lowering its head, then raising the head can become a valuable appeasement gesture. If an attacker erects its hair, then compressing it will serve as a submission device. In certain rare cases a loser will admit defeat by offering a vulnerable area to the attacker. A chimpanzee, for example, will hold out its hand as a gesture of submission, rendering it extremely vulnerable for serious biting. Because an aggressive chimpanzee would never do such a thing, this begging gesture serves to appease the dominant individual.

The second category of appeasement signals operate as remotivating devices. The subordinate animal sends out signals that stimulate a non-aggressive response and, as this wells up inside the attacker, his urge to fight is suppressed and subdued by it. This is done in one of three main ways. A particularly widespread remotivator is the adoption of juvenile food-begging postures. The weaker individual crouches and begs from the dominant one in the infantile posture characteristic of the particular species—a device especially favoured by females when they are being attacked by males. It is often so effective that the male responds by regurgitating some food to the female, who then completes the food-begging ritual by swallowing it. Now in a thoroughly paternal, protective mood, the male loses his aggression and the pair calm down together. This is the basis of courtship feeding in many species, especially with birds, where the early stages of pair-formation involve a great deal of aggression on the part of the male. Another re-motivating activity is the adoption of a female sexual posture by the weaker animal. Regardless of its sex, or its sexual condition, it may suddenly assume the female rump-presentation posture. When it displays towards the attacker in this way, it stimulates a sexual response which damps down the mood of aggression. In such situations, a dominant male *or* female will mount and pseudo-copulate with either a submissive male or a submissive female.

A third form of re-motivation involves the arousal of the mood to groom or be groomed. A great deal of social or mutual grooming goes on in the animal world and it is strongly associated with the calmer, more peaceful moments of community life. The weaker animal may either invite the winner to groom it, or may make signals requesting permission to perform

138

the grooming itself. Monkeys make great use of this device and have a special facial gesture to go with it, consisting of rapidly smacking the lips together—a modified, ritualised version of part of the normal grooming ceremony. When one monkey grooms another it repeatedly pops fragments of skin and other detritus into its mouth, smacking its lips as it does so. By exaggerating the smacking movements and speeding them up, it signals its readiness to perform this duty and frequently manages in this way to suppress the aggression of the attacker and persuade it to relax and allow itself to be groomed. After a while the dominant individual is so lulled by this procedure that the weakling can slip away unharmed.

These, then are the ceremonies and devices by which animals order their aggressive involvements. The phrase 'nature red in tooth and claw' was originally intended to refer to the brutal prey-killing activities of the carnivores, but it has been applied incorrectly in general terms to the whole subject of animal fighting. Nothing could be further from the truth. If a species is to survive, it simply cannot afford to go around slaughtering its own kind. Intra-specific aggression has to be inhibited and controlled, and the more powerful and savage the prey-killing weapons of a particular species are, the stronger must be the inhibitions about using them to settle disputes with rivals. This is the 'law of the jungle' where territorial and hierarchy disagreements are concerned. Those species that failed to obey this law have long since become extinct.

How do we, as a species, measure up to this situation? What is our own special repertoire of threatening and appeasing signals? What are our fighting methods, and how do we control them?

Aggressive arousal produces in us all the same physiological upheavals and muscular tensions and agitations that were described in the general animal context. Like other species, we also show a variety of displacement activities. In some respects we are not as well equipped as other species to develop these basic responses into powerful signals. We cannot intimidate our opponents, for example, by erecting our body hair. We still do it in moments of great shock ('My hair stood on end'), but as a signal it is of little use. In other respects we can do much better. Our very nakedness, which prevents us from bristling effectively, gives us the chance to send powerful flushing and paling signals. We can go 'white with rage', 'red with anger', or 'pale with fear'. It is the white colour we have to watch for here: this spells activity. If it is combined with other actions that signal attack, then it is a vital danger signal. If it is combined with other actions that signal fear, then it is a panic signal. It is caused, you will recall, by the activation of the sympathetic nervous system, the 'go' system, and it is not to be treated lightly. The reddening, on the other hand, is less worrying: it is caused by the frantic counter-balancing attempts of the parasympathetic system, and indicates that the 'go' system is already being undermined. The angry, red-faced opponent who faces you is far less likely to attack than the white-faced, tight-lipped one. Red-face's conflict is such that he is all bottled up and inhibited, but white-face is still ready for action. Neither can be trifled with, but white-face is much more likely to spring in to the attack unless he is immediately appeased or counter-threatened even more strongly.

In a similar vein, rapid deep breathing is a danger signal, but it has already become less of a threat when it develops into irregular snorts and gurgles. The same relationship exists between the dry mouth of incipient attack and the slobbering mouth of the more intensely inhibited assault. Urination, defecation and fainting usually arrive a little later on the scene, following in the wake of the massive shock-wave that accompanies moments of immense tension.

When the urge to attack and escape are both strongly activated simultaneously, we exhibit a number of characteristic intention movements and ambivalent posturings. The most familiar of these is the raising of a clenched fist—a gesture that has become ritualised in two ways. It is performed at some distance from the opponent, at a point where it is too far away to be carried through into a blow. Thus its function is no longer mechanical; instead it has become a visual signal. (With the arm bent and held sideways it has now become the defiant formalised gesture of communist regimes.) It has become further ritualised by the addition of back-and-forth striking movements of the forearm. Fist-shaking of this kind is again visual rather than mechanical in its impact. We perform rhythmically repeated 'blows' with the fist, but still at a safe distance.

While doing this, the whole body may make short approach-intention movements, actions which repeatedly check themselves from going too far. The feet may be stamped forcibly and loudly and the fist brought down and thumped on any near-by object. This last action is an example of something seen frequently in other animals, where it is referred to as a redirection activity. What happens is that, because the object (the opponent) stimulating the attack is too frightening to be directly assaulted, the aggressive movements are released, but have to be re-directed towards some other, less intimidating object, such as a harmless bystander (we have all suffered from this at one time or another), or even an inanimate object. If the latter is used it may be viciously pulverised or destroyed. When a wife smashes a vase to the floor, it is, of course, really her husband's head that lies there broken into small pieces. It is interesting that chimpanzees and gorillas frequently perform their own versions of this display, when they tear up, smash, and throw around branches and vegetation. Again, it has a powerful visual impact.

A specialised and important accompaniment to all these aggressive displays is the making of threatening facial expressions. These, along with our verbalised vocal signals, provide our most precise method of communicating our exact aggressive mood. Although our smiling face, discussed in an earlier chapter, is unique to our species, our aggressive faces, expressive though they may be, are much the same as those of all the other higher primates. (We can tell a fierce monkey or a scared monkey at a glance, but we have to learn the friendly monkey face.) The rules are quite simple: the more the urge to attack dominates the urge to flee, the more the face pulls itself forwards. When the reverse is the case and fear gets the upper hand, then all the facial details are pulled back. In the attack face, the eyebrows are brought forward in a frown, the forehead is smooth, the mouth-corners are held forward, and the lips make a tight, pursed line. As fear comes to dominate the mood, a scared-threat face appears. The eyebrows are raised, the forehead wrinkles, the mouth-corners are pulled back and the lips part, exposing the teeth. This face often accompanies other gestures that appear to be very aggressive, and such things as forehead-wrinkling and teeth-baring are sometimes thought of as 'fierce' signals because of this. But in fact they are fear signs, the face providing an early-warning signal that fear is very much present, despite the persistence of intimidating gestures by the rest of the body. It is still, of course, a threatening face and cannot be treated smugly. If full fear were being expressed, the face-pulling would be abandoned and the opponent would be retreating.

All this face-making we share with the monkeys, a fact that is worth remembering if ever you come face to face with a large baboon, but there are other faces that we have invented culturally, such as sticking out the tongue, puffing out the cheeks, thumbing the nose, and exaggeratedly screwing up the features, that add considerably to our threat repertoire. Most cultures have also added a variety of threatening or insulting gestures employing the rest of the body. Aggressive intention movements ('hopping mad') have been elaborated into violent war dances, of many different and highly stylised kinds. The function here has become communal arousal and synchronisation of strong aggressive feelings, rather than direct visual display to the enemy.

Because, with the cultural development of lethal artificial weapons, we have become such a potentially dangerous species, it is not surprising to find that we have an extraordinarily wide range of appeasement signals. We share with the other primates the basic submissive response of crouching and screaming. In addition we have formalised a whole variety of subordinating displays. Crouching itself has become extended into grovelling and prostrating. Minor intensities of it are expressed in the form of kneeling, bowing and curtsying. The key signal here is the lowering of the body in relation to the dominant individual. When threatening, we puff ourselves up to our greatest height, making our bodies as tall and as large as possible. Submissive behaviour must therefore take the opposite course and bring the body down as far as possible. Instead of doing this in a random way, we have stylised it at a number of characteristic, fixed stages, each with its own special signal meaning. The act of saluting is interesting in this context, because it shows how far from the original gesture formalisation can carry our cultural signs. At first sight a military salute looks like an aggressive movement. It is similar to the signal version of raising-an-arm-to-strike-a-blow. The vital difference is that the hand is not clenched and it points towards the cap or hat. It is, of course, a stylised modification of the act of removing the hat, which itself was originally part of the procedure of lowering the height of the body.

The distillation of the bowing movement from the original, crude, primate crouch is also interesting. The key feature here is the lowering of the eyes. A direct stare is typical of the most out-and-out aggression. It is part of the fiercest facial expressions and accompanies all the most belligerent gestures. (This is why the children's game of 'stare you out' is so difficult to perform and why the simple curiosity staring of a young child—'It's rude to stare'—is so condemned.) No matter how reduced in extent the bow becomes by social custom, it always retains the face-lowering element. Male members of a royal court, for example, who, through constant repetition, have modified their bowing reactions, still lower the face, but instead of bending from the waist they now bow stiffly from the neck, lowering only the head region.

On less formal occasions the anti-stare response is given by simple looking-away movements, or a 'shifty-eyed' expression. Only a truly aggressive individual can fix you in the eye for any length of time. During ordinary face-to-face conversations we typically look away from our companions when we are talking, then glance back at them at the end of each sentence, or

143

'paragraph', to check their response to what we have said. A professional lecturer takes some time to train himself to look directly at the members of his audience, instead of over their heads, down at his rostrum, or out towards the side or back of the hall. Even thought he is in such a dominant position, there are so many of them, all staring (from the safety of their seats) at him, that he experiences a basic and initially uncontrollable fear of them. Only after a great deal of practice can he overcome this. The simple, aggressive, physical act of being stared at by a large group of people is also the cause of the fluttering 'butterflies' in the actor's stomach before he makes his entrance on to the stage. He has all his intellectual worries about the qualities of his performance and its reception, of course, but the massed threat-stare is an additional and more fundamental hazard for him. (This is again a case of the curiosity stare being confused at an unconscious level with the threat-stare.) The wearing of spectacles and sunglasses makes the face appear more aggressive because it artificially and accidentally enlarges the pattern of the stare. If we are looked at by someone wearing glasses, we are being given a super-stare. Mild-mannered individuals tend to select thin-rimmed or rimless spectacles (probably without realising why they do so), because this enables them to see better with the minimum of stare exaggeration. In this way they avoid arousing counter-aggression.

A more intense form of anti-stare is covering the eyes with the hands, or burying the face in the crook of the elbow. The simple act of closing the eyes also cuts off the stare, and it is intriguing that certain individuals compulsively and repeatedly shut their eyes briefly whilst facing and talking to strangers. It is as though their normal blinking responses have become lengthened into extended eye-masking moments. The response vanishes when they are conversing with close friends in a situation where they feel at ease. Whether they are trying to shut off the 'threatening' presence of the stranger, or whether they are attempting to reduce their staring rate, or both, is not always clear.

Because of their powerful intimidating affect, many species have evolved staring eye-spots as self-defence mechanisms. Many moths have a pair of startling eye-markings on their wings. These lie concealed until the creatures are attacked by predators. The wings then open and flash the bright eye-spots in the face of the enemy. It has been proved experimentally that this exerts a valuable intimidating influence on the would-be killers, who frequently flee and leave the insects unmolested. Many fish and some species of birds and even mammals have adopted this technique. In our own species, commercial products have sometimes used the same device (perhaps knowingly, perhaps not). Motor-car designers employ headlamps in this way and frequently add to the overall aggressive impression by sculpturing the line of the front of the bonnet into the shape of a frown. In addition they add 'bared teeth' in the form of a metal grille between the 'eye-spots'. As the roads have become increasingly crowded and driving an increasingly belligerent activity, the threat-faces of cars have become progressively improved and refined, imparting to their drivers a more and more aggressive image. On a smaller scale certain products have been given threat-face brand names, such as OXO, OMO, OZO, and OVO. Fortunately for the manufacturers, these do not repel customers: on the contrary, they catch the eye and, having caught it, reveal themselves to be no more than harmless cardboard boxes. But the impact has already been drawn to *that* product rather than to its rivals.

I mentioned earlier that chimpanzees appease by holding out a limp hand towards the dominant individual. We share this gesture with them, in the form of the typical begging or imploring posture. We have also adapted it as a widespread greeting gesture in the shape of the friendly hand-shake. Friendly gestures often grow out of submissive ones. We saw earlier how this happened with the smiling and laughing responses (both of which, incidentally, still appear in appeasing situations as the timid smile and the nervous titter). Handshaking occurs as a mutual ceremony between individuals of more or less equal rank, but is transformed into bowing to kiss the held hand when there is strong inequality between the ranks. (With increasing 'equality' between the sexes and the various classes, this latter refinement is now becoming rarer, but still persists in certain specialised spheres where formal dominance hierarchies are rigidly adhered to, as in the case of the Church.) In certain instances hand-shaking has become modified into self-shaking or hand-wringing. In some cultures this is the standard greet-ing appeasement, in others it is performed only in more extreme 'imploring' contexts.

There are many other cultural specialities in the realm of submissive behaviour, such as throwing in the towel or showing the white flag, but these need not concern us here. One or two of the simpler re-motivat-ing devices do, however, deserve a mention, if only because they bear an interesting relationship to similar patterns in other species. You will recall that certain juvenile, sexual or grooming patterns were performed towards aggressive or potentially aggressive individuals as a method of arousing non-aggressive feelings that competed with the more violent ones and suppressed them. In our own species, juvenile behaviour on the part of submissive adults is particularly common dur-ing courtship. The courting pair often adopt 'baby-talk', not because they are heading towards parentalism themselves, but because it arouses tender, protective maternal or paternal feelings in the partner and there-by suppresses more aggressive feelings (or, for that matter, more fearful ones). It is amusing, when think-ing back to the development of this pattern into court-ship-feeding in birds, to notice the extraordinary increase in mutual feeding that goes on in our own courtship phase. At no other time in our lives do we devote so much effort to popping tasty morsels into one another's mouths, or offering one another boxes of chocolates.

As regards re-motivation in a sexual direction, this occurs wherever a subordinate (male or female) adopts a generalised attitude of 'femininity' towards a domin-ant individual (male or female) in an aggressive rather than a truly sexual context. This is widespread, but the more specific case of the adoption of the female sexual rump-presentation posture as an appeasement gesture has virtually vanished, along with the dis-appearance of the original sexual posture itself. It is largely confined now to a form of schoolboy punishment, with rhythmic whipping replacing the rhythmic pelvic thrusts of the dominant male. It is doubtful whether schoolmasters would persist in this practice if they fully appreciated the fact that, in reality, they were performing an ancient primate form of ritual copulation with their pupils. They could just as well inflict pain on their victims without forcing them to adopt the bent-over submissive female posture. (It is significant that schoolgirls are rarely, if ever, beaten in this way—the sexual origins of the act would then become too obvious.) It has been imaginatively suggested by one authority that the reason for sometimes forcing schoolboys to lower their trousers for the administration of the punishment is not related to increasing the pain, but rather to enabling the dominant male to witness the reddening of the buttocks as the beating proceeds, which so vividly recalls the flushing of the primate female hindquarters when in full sexual condition. Whether this is so or not, one thing is certain about this extraordinary ritual, namely that as a re-motivating appeasement device it is a dismal failure. The more the unfortunate schoolboy stimulates the dominant male crypto-sexually, the more likely he is to perpetuate the ritual and, because the rhythmic pelvic thrusts have become symbolically modified into rhythmic blows of the cane, the victim is right back where he started. He has managed to switch a direct attack into a sexual one, but has then been double-crossed by the symbolic conversion of this sexual one back into another aggressive pattern.

The third re-motivating device, that of grooming, plays a minor, but useful role in our species. We frequently employ stroking and patting movements to soothe an agitated individual, and many of the more dominant members of society spend long hours having themselves groomed and fussed over by subordinates. But we shall return to this subject in another chapter.

Displacement activities also play a part in our aggressive encounters, appearing in almost any situation of stress or tension. We differ from other animals, however, in that we do not restrict ourselves to a few species-typical displacement patterns. We make use of virtually any trivial actions as outlets for our pent-up feelings. In an agitated state of conflict we may arrange ornaments, light a cigarette, clean our spectacles, glance at a wrist-watch, pour a drink, or nibble a piece of food. Any of these actions may, of course, be performed for normal functional reasons, but in their displacement activity roles they no longer serve these functions. The ornaments that are rearranged were already adequately displayed. They were not in a muddle and may, indeed, be in a worse state after their agitated rearrangement. The cigarette that is lit in a tense moment may be started when a perfectly good and unfinished one has just been nervously stubbed out. Also, the rate of smoking during tension bears no relation to the physiological addictive nicotine demands of the system. The spectacles that are so laboriously polished are already clean. The watch that is wound up so vigorously does not need winding, and when we glance at it our eyes do not even register what times it tells. When we sip a displacement drink it is not because we are thirsty. When we nibble displacement food it is not because we are hungry. All these actions are performed, not for the normal rewards they bring, but simply for the sake of doing something in an attempt to relieve the tension. They occur with particularly high frequency during the initial stages of social encounters, where hidden fears and aggressions are lurking just below the surface. At a dinner party, or any small social gathering, as soon as the mutual appeasement ceremonies of hand-shaking and smiling are over, displacement cigarettes, displacement drinks and displacement food-snacks are immediately offered. Even at large-scale entertainments such as the theatre and cinema the flow of events is deliberately broken up by short intervals when the audience can indulge in brief bouts of their favourite displacement activities.

When we are in more intense moments of aggressive tension, we tend to revert to displacement activities of a kind that we share with other primate species, and our outlets become more primitive. A chimpanzee in

148

such a situation can be seen to perform repeated and agitated scratching movements, which are of a rather special kind and different from the normal response to an itch. It is confined largely to the head region, or sometimes the arms. The movements themselves are rather stylised. We behave in much the same way, performing stilted displacement grooming actions. We scratch our heads, bite our nails, 'wash' our faces with our hands, tug at our beards or moustaches if we have them, or adjust our coiffure, rub, pick, sniff or blow our noses, stroke our ear-lobes, clean our ear-passages, rub our chins, lick our lips, or rub our hands together in a rinsing action. If moments of great conflict are studied carefully, it can be observed that these activities are all carried out in a ritual fashion without the careful localised adjustments of the true cleaning actions. The displacement head-scratch of one individual may differ markedly from its equivalent in another, but each scratcher develops his own rather fixed and characteristic way of doing it. As real cleaning is not involved, it is of little importance that one region gets all the attention while others are ignored. In any social interaction between a small group of individuals the subordinate members of the group can easily be identified by the higher frequency of their displacement self-grooming activities. The truly dominant individual can be recognised by the almost complete absence of such actions. If the ostensibly dominant member of the group does, in fact, perform a larger number of small displacement activities, then this means that his official dominance is being threatened in some way by the other individuals present.

In discussing all these aggressive and submissive behaviour patterns, it has been assumed that the individuals concerned have been 'telling the truth' and have not been consciously and deliberately modifying their actions to achieve special ends. We 'lie' more with our words than our other communication signals, but even so the phenomenon cannot be overlooked entirely. It is extremely difficult to 'utter' untruths with the kind of behaviour patterns we have been discussing, but not impossible. As I have already mentioned, when parents adopt this procedure towards their young children, it usually fails much more drastically than they realise. Between adults, however, who are much more preoccupied with the verbalised information content of the social interactions, it can be more successful. Unfortunately for the behaviour-liar, he typically lies only with certain selected elements of his total signalling system. Others, which he is not aware of, give the game away. The most successful behaviour-liars are those who, instead of consciously concentrating on modifying specific signals, think themselves into the basic mood they wish to convey and then let the small details take care of themselves. This method is frequently used with great success by professional liars, such as actors and actresses. Their entire working lives are spent performing behavioural lies, a process which can sometimes be extremely damaging to their private lives. Politicians and diplomats are also required to perform an undue amount of behavioural lying, but unlike the actors they are not socially 'licensed to lie', and the resultant guilt feelings tend to interfere with their performances. Also, unlike the actors, they do not undergo prolonged training courses.

Even without professional training, it is possible, with a little effort, and a careful study of the facts presented in this book, to achieve the desired effect. I have deliberately tested this out on one or two occasions, with some degree of success, when dealing with the police. I have reasoned that if there is a strong biological tendency to be appeased by submissive gestures, then this predisposition should be open to manipulation if the proper signals are used. Most drivers, when caught by the police for some minor motoring offence, immediately respond by arguing their innocence, or making excuses of some sort for their behaviour. In doing this they are defending their (mobile) territory and are setting themselves up as territorial rivals. This is the worst possible course of action. It forces the police to counter-attack. If, instead, an attitude of abject submission is adopted, it will become increasingly difficult for the police officer to avoid a sensation of appeasement. A total admission of guilt based on sheer stupidity and inferiority puts the policeman into a position of immediate dominance from which it is difficult for him to attack. Gratitude and admiration must be expressed for the efficiency of his action in stopping you. But words are not enough. The appropriate postures and gestures must be added. Fear and submission in both body posture and facial expression must be clearly demonstrated. Above all, it is essential to get quickly out of the car and move away from it towards the policeman. He must not be allowed to approach you, or you have forced him to go out of his way and thereby threatened him. Furthermore, by staying in the car you are remaining in your own territory. By moving away from it you are automatically weakening your territorial status. In addition to this, the sitting posture inside the car is an inherently dominant one. The power of the seated position is an unsual element in our behaviour. No one may sit if the 'king' is standing. When the 'king' rises, everyone rises. This is a special exception to the general rule about aggressive verticality, which states that increasing submissiveness goes with decreasing posture-height. By leaving the car you therefore shed both your territorial rights and your dominant seated position, and put yourself into a suitably weakened state for the submissive actions that follow. Having stood up, however, it is important not to brace the body erect, but to crouch, lower the head slightly and generally sag. The tone of voice is as important as the words used. Anxious facial expressions and looking away movements are also valuable and a few displacement self-grooming activities can be added for good measure.

Unfortunately, as a driver of a car, one is in a basically aggressive mood of territorial defence, and it is extremely difficult to lie about this mood. It requires either considerable practice, or a good working knowledge of non-verbal behaviour signals. If you are a little short on personal dominance in your ordinary life, the experience, even when consciously and deliberately designed, may be too unpleasant, and it will be preferable to pay the fine.

Although this is a chapter about fighting behaviour, we have so far only dealt with methods of avoiding actual combat. When the situation does finally deteriorate into physical contact, the naked ape—unarmed—behaves in a way that contrasts interestingly with that seen in other primates. For them the teeth are the most important weapons, but for us it is the hands. Where they grab and bite, we grab and squeeze, or strike out with clenched fists. Only in infants or very young children does biting play a significant role in unarmed combat. They, of course, have not yet been able to develop their arm and hand muscles sufficiently to make a great impact with them.

We can witness adult un-armed combat today in a number of highly stylised versions, such as wrestling, judo and boxing, but in its original, unmodified form it is now rare. The moment that serious combat begins, artificial weapons of one sort or another are brought into play. In their crudest form, these are thrown or used as extensions of the fist for delivering heavy blows. Under special circumstances chimpanzees have been able to extend their attacks this far. In conditions of semi-captivity they have been observed to pick up a branch and slam it down hard on to the body of a stuffed leopard, or to tear up clods of earth and hurl them across a water ditch at passers-by. But there is little evidence that they use these methods to any extent in the wild state, and none at all that they use them on one another during disputes between rivals. Nevertheless, they give us a glimpse of the way we probably began, with artificial weapons being developed primarily as a means of defence against other species and for the killing of prey. Their use in intraspecific fighting was almost certainly a secondary trend, but once the weapons were there, they became available for dealing with any emergency, regardless of the context.

The simplest form of artificial weapon is a hard, solid, but unmodified, natural object of wood or stone. By simple improvements in the shapes of these objects, the crude actions of throwing and hitting became augmented with the addition of spearing, slashing, cutting and stabbing movements.

The next great behavioural trend in attacking methods was the extension of the distance between the attacker and his enemy, and it is this step that has nearly been our undoing. Spears can work at a distance, but their range is too limited. Arrows are better, but they lack accuracy. Guns widen the gap dramatically, but bombs dropped from the sky can be delivered at an even greater range, and ground-to-ground rockets can carry the attacker's 'blow' further still. The outcome of this is that the rivals, instead of being defeated, are indiscriminately destroyed. As I explained earlier, the proper business of intra-specific aggression at a biological level is the subduing and not the killing of the enemy. The final stages of destruction of life are avoided because the enemy either flees or submits. In both cases the aggressive encounter is then over: the dispute is settled. But the moment that attacking is done from such a distance that the appeasement signals of the losers cannot be read by the winners, then violent aggression is going to go raging on. It can only be consummated by a direct confrontation with abject submission, or the enemy's headlong flight. Neither of these can be witnessed in the remoteness of modern aggression, and the result is wholesale slaughter on a scale unheard of in any other species.

Aiding and abetting this mayhem is our specially evolved co-operativeness. When we improved this important trait in connection with hunting prey, it served us well, but it has now recoiled upon us. The strong urge towards mutual assistance to which it gave rise has become susceptible to powerful arousal in intra-specific aggressive contexts. Loyalty on the hunt has become loyalty in fighting, and war is born. Ironically, it is the evolution of a deep-seated urge to help our fellows that has been the main cause of all the major horrors of war. It is this that has driven us on and given us our lethal gangs, mobs, hordes and armies. Without it they would lack cohesion and aggression would once again become 'personalised'.

It has been suggested that because we evolved as specialised prey-killers, we automatically became rival-killers, and that there is an inborn urge within us to murder our opponents. The evidence, as I have already explained, is against this. Defeat is what an animal wants, not murder; domination is the goal of aggression, not destruction, and basically we do not seem to differ from other species in this respect. There is no good reason why we should. What has happened, however, is that because of the vicious combination of attack remoteness and group co-operativeness, the original goal has become blurred for the individuals involved in the fighting. They attack now more to support their comrades than to dominate their enemies, and their inherent susceptibility to direct appeasement is given little or no chance to express itself. This unfortunate development may yet prove to be our undoing and lead to the rapid extinction of the species.

Not unnaturally, this dilemma has given rise to a great deal of displacement head scratching. A favour ite solution is massive mutual disarmament; but to be effective this would have to be carried to an almost impossible extreme, one that would ensure that all future fighting was carried out as close-contact combat where the automatic, direct appeasement signals could come into operation again. Another solution is to de-patriotise the members of the different social groups; but this would be working against a fundamental biological feature of our species. As fast as alliances could be forged in one direction, they would be broken in another. The natural tendency to form social in-groups could never be eradicated without a major genetical change in our make-up, and one which would automatically cause our complex social structure to disintegrate.

A third solution is to provide and promote harmless, symbolic substitutes for war; but if these really are harmless they will inevitably only go a very small way towards resolving the real problem. It is worth remembering here that this problem, at a biological level, is one of group territorial defence and, in view of the gross overcrowding of our species, also one of group territorial expansion. No amount of boisterous international football is going to solve this.

A fourth solution is the improvement of intellectual control over aggression. It is argued that, since our intelligence has got us into this mess, it is our intelligence that must get us out. Unhappily, where matters as basic as territorial defence are concerned, our higher brain centres are all too susceptible to the urgings of our lower ones. Intellectual control can help us just so far, but no further. In the last resort it is unreliable, and a single, unreasoned, emotional act can undo all the good it has achieved.

The only sound biological solution to the dilemma is massive de-population, or a rapid spread of the species on to other planets, combined if possible with assistance from all four of the courses of action already mentioned. We already know that if our populations go on increasing at their present terrifying rate, uncontrollable aggressiveness will become dramatically increased. This has been proved conclusively with laboratory experiments. Gross overcrowding will produce social stresses and tensions that will shatter our community organisations long before it starves us to death. It will work directly against improvements in intellectual control and will savagely heighten the likelihood of emotional explosion. Such a development can be prevented only by a marked drop in the breeding rate. Unfortunately there are two serious snags here. As already explained, the family unit—which is still the basic unit of all our societies—is a rearing device. It has evolved into its present, advanced and complex state as a system for producing, protecting and maturing offspring. If this function is seriously curtailed or temporarily eliminated, the pair-bonding pattern will suffer, and this will bring its own brand of social chaos. If, on the other hand, a selective attempt is made to stem the breeding flood, with certain pairs permitted to breed freely and others prevented from doing so, then this will work against the essential co-operativeness of society.

What it amounts to, in simple numerical terms, is that if all adult members of the population form pairs and breed, they can only afford to produce two offspring per pair if the community is to be maintained at a steady level. Each individual will then, in effect, be replacing him- or herself. Allowing for the fact that a small percentage of the population already fails to mate and breed, and that there will always be a number of premature deaths from accidental injury or other causes, the average family size can, in fact, be slightly larger. Even so, this will put a heavier burden on the pair-bond mechanism. The lighter offspring-load will mean that greater efforts will have to be made in other directions to keep the pair-bonds tightly tied. But this is a much smaller hazard, in the long term, than the alternative of suffocating overcrowding.

To sum up then, the best solution for ensuring world peace is the widespread promotion of contraception or abortion. Abortion is a drastic measure and can involve serious emotional disturbance. Furthermore, once a zygote has been formed by the act of fertilisation it constitutes a new individual member of society, and its destruction is, in effect, an act of aggression, which is the very pattern of behaviour that we are attempting to control. Contraception is obviously preferable, and any religious or other 'moralising' factions that oppose it must face the fact that they are engaged in dangerous war-mongering.

Having brought up the question of religion, it is perhaps worthwhile taking a closer look at this strange pattern of animal behaviour, before going on to deal with other aspects of the aggressive activities of our species. It is not an easy subject to deal with, but as zoologists we must do our best to observe what actually happens rather than listen to what is supposed to be happening. If we do this, we are forced to the conclusion that, in a behavioural sense, religious activities consist of the coming together of large groups of people to perform repeated and prolonged submissive displays to appease a dominant individual. The dominant individual concerned takes many forms in different cultures, but always has the common factor of immense power. Sometimes it takes the shape of an animal from another species, or an idealised version of it. Sometimes it is pictured more as a wise and elderly member of our own species. Sometimes it becomes more abstract and is referred to as simply as 'the state', or in other such terms. The submissive responses to it may consist of closing the eyes, lowering the head, clasping the hands together in a begging gesture, kneeling, kissing the ground, or even extreme prostration, with the frequent accompaniment of wailing or chanting vocalisations. If these submissive actions are successful, the dominant individual is appeased. Because its powers are so great, the appeasement ceremonies have to be performed at regular and frequent intervals, to prevent its anger from rising again. The dominant individual is usually, but not always, referred to as a god.

Since none of these gods exist in a tangible form, why have they been invented? To find the answer to this we have to go right back to our ancestral origins. Before we evolved into co-operative hunters, we must have lived in social groups of the type seen today in other species of apes and monkeys. There, in typical cases, each group is dominated by a single male. He is the boss, the overlord, and every member of the group has to appease him or suffer the consequences. He is also most active in protecting the group from outside hazards and in settling squabbles between lesser members. The whole life of a member of such a group revolves around the dominant animal. His all-powerful role gives him a god-like status. Turning now to our immediate ancestors, it is clear that, with the growth of the co-operative spirit so vital for successful group hunting, the application of the dominant individual's authority had to be severely limited if he was to retain the active, as opposed to passive, loyalty of the other group members. They had to want to help him instead of simply fear him. He had to become more 'one of them'. The old-style monkey tyrant had to go, and in his place there arose a more tolerant, more co-operative naked ape leader. This step was essential for the new type of 'mutual-aid' organisation that was evolving, but it gave rise to a problem. The total dominance of the Number 1 member of the group having been replaced by a qualified dominance, he could no longer command unquestioning allegiance. This change in the order of things, vital as it was to the new social system, nevertheless left a gap. From our ancient background there remained a need for an all-powerful figure who could keep the group under control, and the vacancy was filled by the invention of a god. The influence of the invented god-figure could then operate as a force additional to the now more restricted influence of the group leader.

At first sight, it is surprising that religion has been so successful, but its extreme potency is simply a measure of the strength of our fundamental biological tendency, inherited directly from our monkey and ape ancestors, to submit ourselves to an all-powerful, dominant member of the group. Because of this, religion has proved immensely valuable as a device for aiding social cohesion, and it is doubtful whether our species could have progressed far without it, given the unique combination of circumstances of our evolutionary origins. It has led to a number of bizarre by-products, such as a belief in 'another life' where we will at last meet up with the god figures. They were, for reasons already explained, unavoidably detained from joining us in the present life, but this omission can be corrected in an after-life. In order to facilitate this, all kinds of strange practices have been developed in connection with the disposal of our bodies when we die. If we are going to join our dominant overlords, we must be well prepared for the occasion and elaborate burial ceremonies must be performed.

Religion has also given rise to a great deal of unnecessary suffering and misery, wherever it has become over-formalised in its application, and whenever the professional 'assistants' of the god figures have been unable to resist the temptation to borrow a little of his power and use it themselves. But despite its chequered history it is a feature of our social life that we cannot do without. Whenever it becomes unacceptable, it is quietly, or sometimes violently, rejected, but in no time at all it is back again in a new form, carefully disguised perhaps, but containing all the same old basic elements. We simply have to 'believe in something'. Only a common belief will cement us together and keep us under control. It could be argued that, on this basis, any belief will do, so long as it is powerful enough; but this is not strictly true. It must be impressive and it must be seen to be impressive. Our communal nature demands the performance of and participation in elaborate group ritual. Elimination of the 'pomp and circumstance' will leave a terrible cultural gap and the indoctrination will fail to operate properly at the deep, emotional level so vital to it. Also, certain types of belief are more wasteful and stultifying than others and can side-track a community into rigidifying patterns of behaviour that hamper its qualitative development. As a species we are a predominantly intelligent and exploratory animal, and beliefs harnessed to this fact will be the most beneficial for us. A belief in the validity of the acquisition of knowledge and a scientific understanding of the world we live in, the creation and appreciation of aesthetic phenomena in all their many forms, and the broadening and deepening of our range of experiences in day-to-day living, is rapidly becoming the 'religion' of our time. Experience and understanding are our rather abstract god-figures, and ignorance and stupidity will make them angry. Our schools and universities are our religious training centres, our libraries, museums, art galleries, theatres, concert halls and sports arenas are our places of communal worship. At home we worship with our books, newspapers, magazines, radios and television sets. In a sense, we still believe in an after-life, because part of the reward obtained from our creative works is the feeling that, through them, we will 'live on' after we are dead. Like all religions, this one has its dangers, but if we have to have one, and it seems that we do, then it certainly appears to be the one most suitable for the unique biological qualities of our species. Its adoption by an ever growing majority of the world population can serve as a compensating and reassuring source of optimism to set against the pessimism expressed earlier concerning our immediate future as a surviving species.

Before we embarked on this religious discourse, we had been examining the nature of only one aspect of the organisation of aggressiveness in our species, namely the group defence of a territory. But as I explained at the beginning of this chapter, the naked ape is an animal with three distinct social forms of aggression, and we must now consider the other two. They are the territorial defence of the family-unit within the larger group-unit, and the personal individual maintenance of hierarchy positions.

The spatial defence of the home site of the family unit has remained with us through all our massive architectural advances. Even our largest buildings, when designed as living-quarters, are assiduously divided into repetitive units, one per family. There has been little or no architectural 'division of labour'. Even the introduction of communal eating or drinking buildings, such as restaurants and bars, has not eliminated the inclusion of dining-rooms in the family-unit quarters. Despite all the other advances, the design of our cities and towns is still dominated by our ancient, naked-ape need to divide our groups up into small, discrete, family territories. Where houses have not yet been squashed up into blocks of flats, the defended area is carefully fenced, walled, or hedged off from its neighbours, and the demarcation lines are rigidly respected and adhered to, as in other territorial species.

One of the important features of the family territory is that it must be easily distinguished in some way from all the others. Its separate location gives it a uniqueness, of course, but this is not enough. Its shape and general appearance must make it stand out as an easily identifiable entity, so that it can become the 'personalised' property of the family that lives there. This is something which seems obvious enough, but which has frequently been overlooked or ignored, either as a result of economic pressures, or the lack of biological awareness of architects. Endless rows of uniformly repeated, identical houses have been erected in cities and towns all over the world. In the case of blocks of flats the situation is even more acute. The psychological damage done to the territorialism of the families forced by architects, planners and builders to live under these conditions is incalculable. Fortunately, the families concerned can impose territorial uniqueness on their dwellings in other ways. The buildings themselves can be painted different colours. The gardens, where there are any, can be planted and landscaped in individual styles. The insides of the houses or flats can be decorated and filled with ornaments, bric-à-brac and personal belongings

160

in profusion. This is usually explained as being done to make the place 'look nice'. In fact, it is the exact equivalent to another territorial species depositing its personal scent on a landmark near its den. When you put a name on a door, or hang a painting on a wall, you are, in dog or wolf terms, for example, simply cocking your leg on them and leaving your personal mark there. Obsessive 'collecting' of specialised categories of objects occurs in certain individuals who, for some reason, experience an abnormally strong need to define their home territories in this way.

Bearing this in mind, it is amusing to note the large number of cars that contain small mascots and other personal identification symbols, or to watch the business executive moving into a new office and immediately setting out on his desk his favourite personal pen-tray, paper-weight and perhaps a photograph of his wife. The motor-car and the business office are sub-territories, offshoots of his home base, and it is a great relief to be able to cock his leg on these as well, making them into more familiar, 'owned' spaces.

This leaves us with the question of aggression in relation to the social dominance hierarchy. The individual, as opposed to the places he frequents, must also be defended. His social status must be maintained and, if possible improved, but it must be done cautiously, or he will jeopardise his co-operative contacts. This is where all the subtle aggressive and submissive signalling described earlier comes in to play. Group co-operativeness demands and gets a high degree of conformity in both dress and behaviour, but within the bounds of this conformity there is still great scope for hierarchy competitiveness. Because of these conflicting demands it reaches almost incredible degrees of subtlety. The exact form of the knotting of a tie, the precise arrangement of the exposed section of a breast-pocket handkerchief, minute distinctions in vocal accent, and other such seemingly trivial characteristics, take on a vital social significance in determining the social standing of the individual. An experienced member of society can read them off at a glance. He would be totally at a loss to do so if suddenly jettisoned into the social hierarchy of New

Guinea tribesmen, but in his own culture he is rapidly forced to become an expert. In themselves these tiny differences of dress and habit are utterly meaningless, but in relation to the game of juggling for position and holding it in the dominance hierarchy they are all-important.

We did not evolve, of course, to live in huge conglomerations of thousands of individuals. Our behaviour is designed to operate in small tribal groups probably numbering well under a hundred individuals. In such situations every member of the tribe will be known personally to every other member, as is the case with other species of apes and monkeys today. In this type of social organisation it is easy enough for the dominance hierarchy to work itself out and become stabilised, with only gradual changes as members become older and die. In a massive city community the situation is much more stressful. Every day exposes the urbanite to sudden contacts with countless strangers, a situation unheard-of in any other primate species. It is impossible to enter into personal hierarchy relationships with all of them, although this would be the natural tendency. Instead they are allowed to go scurrying by, undominated and undominating. In order to facilitate this lack of social contact, anti-touching behaviour patterns develop. This has already been mentioned when dealing with sexual behaviour, where one sex accidentally touches another, but it applies to more than simply the avoidance of sexual behaviour. It covers the whole range of social-relationship initiation. By carefully avoiding staring at one another, gesturing in one another's direction, signalling in any way, or making physical bodily contact, we manage to survive in an otherwise impossibly overstimulating social situation. If the no-touching rule is broken, we immediately apologise to make it clear that it was purely accidental.

Anti-contact behaviour enables us to keep our number of acquaintances down to the correct level for our species. We do this with remarkable consistency and uniformity. If you require confirmation, take the address or phone books of a hundred widely different types of city-dwellers and count up the number of personal acquaintances listed there. You will find that nearly all of them know well about the same number of individuals, and that this number approximates to what we would think of as a small tribal group. In other words, even in our social encounters we are obeying the basic biological rules of our ancient ancestors.

There will of course be exceptions to this rule—individuals who are professionally concerned with making large numbers of personal contacts, people with behaviour defects that make them abnormally shy or lonely, or people whose special psychological problems render them unable to obtain the expected social rewards from their friends and who try to compensate for this by frantic 'socialising' in all directions. But these types account for only a small proportion of the town and city populations. All the rest happily go about their business in what seems to be a great seething mass of bodies, but which is in reality an incredibly complicated series of interlocking and overlapping tribal groups. How little, how very little, the naked ape has changed since his early, primitive days.

CHAPTER SIX

FEEDING

THE feeding behaviour of the naked ape appears at first sight to be one of his most variable, opportunistic, and culturally susceptible activities, but even here there are a number of basic biological principles at work. We have already taken a close look at the way his ancestral fruit-picking patterns had to become modified into co-operative prey-killing. We have seen how this led to a number of fundamental changes in his feeding routine. Food-seeking had to become more elaborate and carefully organised. The urge to kill prey had to become partially independent of the urge to eat. Food was taken to a fixed home base for consumption. Greater food preparation had to be carried out. Meals became larger and more spaced out in time. The meat component of the diet became dramatically increased. Food storage and food sharing was practised. Food had to be provided by the males for their family units. Defecation activities had to be controlled and modified.

All these changes were taking place over a very long period of time, and it is significant that, despite the great technological advances of recent years, we are still faithful to them. It would seem that they are rather more than mere cultural devices, to be buffeted this way and that by the whims of fashion. Judging by our present-day behaviour, they must, to some extent at any rate, have become deep-seated biological characteristics of our species.

As we have already noted, the improved food-collecting techniques of modern agriculture have left the majority of the adult males in our societies without a hunting role. They compensate for this by going out to 'work'. Working has replaced hunting, but has retained many of its basic characteristics. It involves a regular trip from the home base to the 'hunting' grounds. It is a predominantly masculine pursuit, and provides opportunities for male-to-male interaction and group activity. It involves taking risks and planning strategies. The pseudo-hunter speaks of 'making a killing in the City'. He becomes ruthless in his dealings. He is said to be 'bringing home the bacon'.

When the pseudo-hunter is relaxing he goes to all-male 'clubs', from which the females are completely excluded. Younger males tend to form into all-male gangs, often 'predatory' in nature. Throughout the whole range of these organisations, from learned societies, social clubs, fraternities, trade unions, sports clubs, masonic groups, secret societies, right down to teenage gangs, there is a strong emotional feeling of male 'togetherness'. Powerful group loyalties are involved. Badges, uniforms and other identification labels are worn. Initiation ceremonies are invariably carried out with new members. The unisexuality of these groupings must not be confused with homosexuality. They have basically nothing to do with sex. They are all primarily concerned with the male-to-male bond of the ancient co-operative hunting group. The important role they play in the lives of the adult males reveals the persistence of the basic, ancestral urges. If this were not so, the activities they promote could just as well be carried on without the elaborate segregation and ritual, and much of it could be done within the sphere of the family units. Females frequently resent the departure of their males to 'join the boys', reacting to it as though it signified some kind of family disloyalty. But they are wrong to do so. All they are witnessing is the modern expression of the age-old male-grouping hunting tendency of the species. It is just as basic as the male-female bonding of the naked ape and, indeed, evolved in close conjunction with it. It will always be with us, at least until there has been some new and major genetic change in our make-up.

Although working has largely replaced hunting today, it has not completely eliminated the more primitive forms of expression of this basic urge. Even where there is no economic excuse for participating in the pursuit of animal prey, this activity still persists in a variety of forms. Big-game hunting, stag-hunting, fox-hunting, coursing, falconry, wild-fowling, angling and the hunting-play of children are all contemporary manifestations of the ancient hunting urge.

It has been argued that the true motivation behind these present-day activities has more to do with the defeating of rivals than the hunting down of prey; that the desperate creature at bay represents the most hated member of our own species, the one we would so like to see in the same situation. There is undoubtedly an element of truth in this, at least for some individuals, but when these patterns of activity are viewed as a whole it is clear that it can provide only a partial explanation. The essence of 'sport-hunting' is that the prey should be given a fair chance of escaping. (If the prey is merely a substitute for a hated rival, then why give him any chance at all?) The whole procedure of sport-hunting involves a deliberately contrived inefficiency, a self-imposed handicap, on the part of the hunters. They could easily use machine-guns, or more deadly weapons, but that would not be 'playing the game'—the hunting game. It is the challenge that counts, the complexities of the chase and the subtle manoeuvres that provide the rewards.

One of the essential features of the hunt is that it is a tremendous gamble and so it is not surprising that gambling, in the many stylised forms it takes today, should have such a strong appeal for us. Like primitive hunting and sport-hunting, it is predominantly a male pursuit and, like them, it is surrounded by seriously observed social rules and rituals.

An examination of our class structure reveals that both sport-hunting and gambling are more the concern of the lower and upper social classes than of the middle classes, and there is a very good reason for this if we accept them as expressions of a basic hunting drive. I pointed out earlier that work has become the major substitute for primitive hunting, but as such it has most benefited the middle classes. For the average lower-class male, the nature of the work he is required to do is poorly suited to the demands of the hunting drive. It is too repetitive, too predictable. It lacks the elements of challenge, luck and risk so essential to the hunting male. For this reason, lower-class males share with the (non-working) upper-class males a greater need to express their hunting urges than do the middle classes, the nature of whose work is much more suited to its role as a hunting substitute.

Leaving hunting and turning now to the next act in the general feeding pattern, we come to the moment of the kill. This element can find a certain degree of expression in the substitute activities of work, sport-hunting and gambling. In sport-hunting the action of killing still occurs in its original form, but in working and gambling contexts it is transformed into moments of symbolic triumph that lack the violence of the physical act. The urge to kill prey is therefore considerably modified in our present day way of life. It keeps reappearing with startling regularity in the playful (and not so playful) activities of young boys, but in the adult world it is subjected to powerful cultural suppression.

Two exceptions to this suppression are (to some extent) condoned. One is the sport-hunting already mentioned, and the other is the spectacle of bull-fighting. Although vast numbers of domesticated animals are slaughtered daily, their killing is normally concealed from the public gaze. With bull-fighting the reverse is the case, huge crowds gathering to watch and experience by proxy the acts of violent prey-killing.

Within the formal limits of blood-sports these activities are permitted to continue, but not without protest. Outside these spheres, all forms of cruelty to animals are forbidden and punished. This has not always been the case. A few hundred years ago the torture and killing of 'prey' was regularly staged as a public entertainment in Britain and many other countries. It has since been recognised that participation in violence of this kind is liable to blunt the sensitivities of the individuals concerned towards all forms of blood-letting. It therefore constitutes a potential source of danger in our complex and crowded societies, where territorial and dominance restrictions can build up to an almost unbearable degree, sometimes finding release in a flood of pent-up aggression of abnormal savagery.

We have so far been dealing with the earlier stages of the feeding sequence and their ramifications. After hunting and killing, we come to the meal itself. As typical primates we ought to find ourselves munching away on small, non-stop snacks. But we are not typical primates. Our carnivorous evolution has modified the whole system. The typical carnivore gorges itself on large meals, well spaced out in time, and we clearly fall in with this pattern. The tendency persists even long after the disappearance of the original hunting pressures that demanded it. Today it would be quite easy for us to revert to our old primate ways if we had the inclination to do so. Despite this, we stick to well-defined feeding times, just as though we were still engaged in active prey-hunting. Few, if any, of the millions of naked apes alive today indulge in the typical scattered feeding routine of the other primates. Even in conditions of plenty, we rarely eat more than three, or at the very most four times a day. For many people, the pattern involves only one or two large daily meals. It could be argued that this is merely a case of cultural convenience, but there is little evidence to support this. It would be perfectly possible, given the complex organisation of food supplies that we now enjoy, to devise an efficient system whereby all food was taken in small snacks, scattered throughout the day. Spreading feeding out in this way could be achieved without any undue loss of efficiency once the cultural pattern became adjusted to it, and it would eliminate the need for the major disruptions in other activities caused by the present 'main meal' system. But, because of our ancient predatory past, it would fail to satisfy our basic biological needs.

It is also revelent to consider the question of why we heat our food and eat it while it is still hot. There are three alternative explanations. One is that it helps to simulate 'prey temperature'. Although we no longer consume freshly killed meat, we nevertheless devour it at much the same temperature as other carnivore species. Their food is hot because it has not yet cooled down: ours is hot because we have re-heated it. An-

168

other interpretation is that we have such weak teeth that we are forced to 'tenderise' the meat by cooking it. But this does not explain why we should want to eat it while it is still hot, or why we should heat up many kinds of food that do not require 'tenderising'. The third explanation is that, by increasing the temperature of the food, we improve its flavour. By adding a complicated range of tasty subsidiaries to the main food objects, we can take this process still further. This relates back, not to our adopted carnivory, but to our more ancient primate past. The foods of typical primates have a much wider variety of flavours than those of carnivores. When a carnivore has gone through its complex sequence of hunting, killing and preparing its food, it behaves much more simply and crudely at the actual crunch. It gobbles; it bolts its food down. Monkeys and apes, on the other hand, are extremely sensitive to the subtleties of varying tastiness in their food morsels. They relish them and keep on moving from one flavour to another. Perhaps, when we heat and spice our meals, we are harking back to this earlier primate fastidiousness. Perhaps this is one way in which we resisted the move towards full-blooded carnivory.

Having raised the question of flavour, there is a misunderstanding that should be cleared up concerning the way we receive these signals. How do we taste what we taste? The surface of the tongue is not smooth, but covered with small projections, called papillae, which carry the taste buds. We each possess approximately 10,000 of these taste buds, but in old age they deteriorate and decrease in number, hence the jaded palate of the elderly gastronome. Surprisingly, we can only respond to four basic tastes. They are: sour, salt, bitter and sweet. When a piece of food is placed on the tongue, we register the proportions of these four properties contained in it, and this blending gives the food its basic flavour. Different areas of the tongue react more strongly to one or other of the four tastes. The tip of the tongue is particularly responsive to salt and sweet, the sides of the tongue to sour and the back of the tongue to bitter. The tongue as a whole can also judge the texture and temperature of the food, but beyond that it cannot go. All the more subtle and varied 'flavours' that we respond to so sensitively are not, in fact, tasted, but smelt. The odour of the food diffuses up into the nasal cavity, where the olfactory membrane is located. When we remark that a particular dish 'tastes' delicious, we are really saying that it tastes and smells delicious. Ironically, when we are suffering from a heavy cold and our sense of smell is severely reduced, we say that our food is tasteless. In reality, we are tasting it as clearly as we ever did. It is its lack of odour that is worrying us.

Having made this point, there is one aspect of our true tasting that requires special comment, and that is our undeniably prevalent 'sweet-tooth'. This is something alien to the true carnivore, but typically primate-like. As the natural food of primates becomes riper and more suitable for consumption, it usually becomes sweeter, and monkeys and apes have a strong reaction to anything that is strongly endowed with this taste. Like other primates, we find it hard to resist 'sweets'. Our ape ancestry expresses itself, despite our strong meat-eating tendency, in the seeking out of specially sweetened substances. We favour this basic taste more than the others. We have 'sweet shops', but no 'sour shops'. Typically, when eating a full-scale meal, we *end* the often complex sequence of flavours with some sweet substance, so that this is the taste that lingers on afterwards. More significantly, when we occasionally take small, inter-meal snacks (and thereby revert, to a slight extent, to an ancient, primate scatter-feeding pattern), we nearly always choose primate sweet food objects, such as candy, chocolate, ice-cream, or sugared drinks.

So powerful is this tendency that it can lead us into difficulties. The point is that there are two elements in a food object that make it attractive to us: its nutritive value and its palatability. In nature, these two factors go hand in hand, but in artificially produced foodstuffs they can be separated, and this can be dangerous. Food objects that are nutritionally almost worthless can be made powerfully attractive simply by adding a large amount of artificial sweetener. If they appeal to our old primate weakness by tasting 'super-sweet', we will lap them up and so stuff ourselves with them that we have little room left for anything else: thus the balance of our diet can be upset. This applies especially in the case of growing children. In an earlier chapter I mentioned recent research which has shown that the preference for sweet and fruity odours falls off dramatically at puberty, when there is a shift in favour of flowery, oily and musky odours. The juvenile weakness for sweetness can be easily exploited, and frequently is.

Adults face another danger. Because their food is in general made so tasty—so much more tasty than it would be in nature—its palatability value rises sharply, and eating responses are overstimulated. The result is in many cases an unhealthy overweight condition. To counteract this, all kinds of bizarre 'dieting' regimes are invented. The 'patients' are told to eat this or that, cut down on this or on that, or to exercise in various ways. Unfortunately there is only one true answer to the problem: to eat less. It works like a charm, but since the subject remains surrounded by super-palatability signals, it is difficult for him, or her, to maintain this course of action for any length of time. The overweight individual is also bedevilled by a further complication. I mentioned earlier the phenomenon of 'displacement activities'—trivial, irrelevant actions performed as tension-relievers in moments of stress. As we saw, a very frequent and common form of displacement activity is 'displacement feeding'. In tense moments we nibble small morsels of food or sip unneeded drinks. This may help to relax the tension in us, but it also helps us to put on weight, especially as the 'trivial' nature of the displacement feeding action usually means that we select for the purpose something sweet. If practised repeatedly over a long period, this leads to the well-known condition of 'fat anxiety', and we can witness the gradual emergence of the familiar, rounded contours of guilt-edged insecurity. For such a person, slimming routines will work only if accompanied by other behavioural changes that reduce the initial state of tension. The role of chewing-gum deserves a mention in this context. This substance appears to have developed exclusively as a displacement feeding device. It provides the necessary tension-relieving 'occupational' element, without contributing damagingly to the overall food intake.

Turning now to the variety of foodstuffs eaten by a present-day group of naked apes, we find that the range is extensive. By and large, primates tend to have a wider range of food objects in their diets than carnivores. The latter have become food specialists, whereas the former are opportunists. Careful field studies of a wild population of Japanese macaque monkeys, for example, have revealed that they consume as many as 119 species of plants, in the shape of buds, shoots, leaves, fruits, roots and barks, not to mention a wide variety of spiders, beetles, butterflies, ants and eggs. A typical carnivore's diet is more nutritious, but also much more monotonous.

When we became killers, we had the best of both worlds. We added meat with a high nutritive value to our diet, but we did not abandon our old primate omnivory. During recent times—that is, during the last few thousand years—food-obtaining techniques have improved considerably, but the basic position remains the same. As far as we can tell, the earliest agricultural systems were of a kind that can loosely be described as 'mixed farming'. The domestication of animals and plants advanced side by side. Even today, with our now immensely powerful dominance over our zoological and botanical environments, we still keep both strings to our bow. What has stopped us from swinging further in one direction or the other? The answer seems to be that, with vastly increasing population densities, an all-out reliance on meat would give rise to difficulties in terms of quantity, whereas an exclusive dependence on crops would be dangerous in terms of quality.

It could be argued that, since our primate ancestors had to make do without a major meat component in their diets, we should be able to do the same. We were driven to become flesh-eaters only by environmental circumstances, and now that we have the environment under control, with elaborately cultivated crops at our disposal, we might be expected to return to our ancient primate feeding patterns. In essence, this is the vegetarian (or, as one cult calls itself, fruitarian) creed, but it has had remarkably little success. The urge to eat meat appears to have become too deep-seated. Given the opportunity to devour flesh, we are loth to relinquish the pattern. In this connection, it is significant that vegetarians seldom explain their chosen diet simply by stating that they prefer it to any other. On the contrary, they construct an elaborate justification for it, involving all kinds of medical inaccuracies and philosophical inconsistencies.

Those individuals who are vegetarian by choice ensure a balanced diet by utilising a wide variety of plant substances, like the typical primates. But for some communities a predominantly meatless diet has become a grim practical necessity rather than an ethical minority-preference. With advancing crop-cultivation techniques and the concentration on a very few staple cereals, a kind of low-grade efficiency has proliferated in certain cultures. The large-scale agricultural operations have permitted the growth of big populations, but their dependency on a few basic cereals has led to serious malnutrition. Such people may breed in large numbers, but they produce poor physical specimens. They survive, but only just. In the same way that abuse of culturally developed weapons can lead to aggressive disaster, abuse of culturally developed feeding techniques can lead to nutritional disaster. Societies that have lost the essential food balance in this way may be able to survive, but they will have to overcome the widespread ill-effects of deficiencies in proteins, minerals and vitamins if they are to progress and develop qualitatively. In all the healthiest and most go-ahead societies today, the meat-and-plant diet balance is well maintained and, despite the dramatic changes that have occurred in the methods of obtaining the nutritional supplies, the progressive naked ape of today is still feeding on much the same basic diet as his ancient hunting ancestors. Once again, the transformation is more apparent than real.

CHAPTER SEVEN

COMFORT

THE place where the environment comes into direct contact with an animal—its body surface—receives a great deal of rough treatment during the course of its life. It is astonishing that it survives the wear and tear and lasts so well. It manages to do so because of its wonderful system of tissue replacement and also because animals have evolved a variety of special comfort movements that help to keep it clean. We tend to think of these cleaning actions as comparatively trivial when considered alongside such patterns as feeding, fighting, fleeing and mating, but without them the body could not function efficiently. For some creatures, such as small birds, plumage maintenance is a matter of life and death. If the feathers are allowed to become bedraggled, the bird will be unable to take off fast enough to avoid its predators and will be unable to keep up its high body temperature if conditions become cold. Birds spend many hours bathing, preening, oiling and scratching themselves and carry out this performance in a long and complicated sequence. Mammals are slightly less complex in their comfort patterns, but nevertheless indulge in a great deal of grooming, licking, nibbling, scratching and rubbing. Like feathers, the hair has to be maintained in good order if it is to keep its owner warm. If it becomes clogged and dirty, it will also increase the risk of disease. Skin parasites have to be attacked and reduced in numbers as far as possible. Primates are no exception to this rule.

In the wild state, monkeys and apes can frequently be seen to groom themselves, systematically working through the fur, picking out small pieces of dried skin or foreign bodies. These are usually popped into the mouth and eaten, or at least tasted. These grooming actions may go on for many minutes, the animal

174

giving an impression of great concentration. The grooming bouts may be interspersed with sudden scratchings or nibblings, directed at specific irritations. Most mammals only scratch with the back foot, but a monkey or ape can use either back or front. Its front limbs are ideally suited to the cleaning tasks. The nimble fingers can run through the fur and locate specific trouble spots with great accuracy. Compared with claws and hooves, the primate's hands are precision 'cleaners'. Even so, two hands are better than one, and this creates something of a problem. The monkey or ape can manage to bring both its hands into play when dealing with its legs, flanks, or front, but cannot really get to grips efficiently in this way with its back, or the arms themselves. Also, lacking a mirror, it cannot see what it is doing when it is concentrating on the head region. Here, it can use both hands, but it must work blind. Obviously, the head, back and arms are going to be less beautifully groomed than the front, sides and legs, unless something special can be done for them.

The solution is social grooming, the development of a friendly mutual aid system. This can be seen in a wide range of both bird and mammal species, but it reaches a peak of expression amongst the higher primates. Special grooming invitation signals have been evolved here and social 'cosmetic' activities are prolonged and intense. When a groomer monkey approaches a groomee monkey, the former signals its intentions to the latter with a characteristic facial expression. It performs a rapid lip-smacking movement, often sticking its tongue out between each smack. The groomee can signal its acceptance of the groomer's approach by adopting a relaxed posture, perhaps offering a particular region of its body to be groomed. As I explained in an earlier chapter the lip-smacking action has evolved as a special ritual out of the repeated particle-tasting movements that take place during a bout of fur-cleaning. By speeding them up and making them more exaggerated and rhythmic, it has been possible to convert them into a conspicuous and unmistakable visual signal.

Because social grooming is a co-operative, non-

175

aggressive activity, the lip-smacking pattern has become a friendly signal. If two animals wish to tighten their bond of friendship, they can do so by repeatedly grooming one another, even if the condition of their fur hardly warrants it. Indeed, there seems to be little relationship today between the amount of dirt on the coat, and the amount of mutual grooming that takes place. Social grooming activities appear to have become almost independent of their original stimuli. Although they still have the vital task of keeping the fur clean, their motivation now appears to be more social than cosmetic. By enabling two animals to stay close together in a non-aggressive, co-operative mood they help to tie tighter the inter-personal bonds between the individuals in the troop or colony.

Out of this friendly signalling system have grown two remotivating devices, one concerned with appeasement and the other with reassurance. If a weak animal is frightened of a stronger one, it can pacify the latter by performing the lip-smacking invitation signal and then proceed to groom its fur. This reduces the aggression of the dominant animal and helps the subordinate one to become accepted. It is permitted to remain 'in the presence' because of services rendered. Conversely, if a dominant animal wishes to calm the fears of a weaker one, it can do so in the same way. By lip-smacking at it, it can underline the fact that it is not aggressive. Despite its dominant aura, it can show that it means no harm. This particular pattern —a reassurance display—is less often seen than the appeasement variety, simply because primate social life requires it less. There is seldom anything that a weak animal has which a dominant might want and could not take by a direct use of aggression. One exception to this can be seen when a dominant but childless female wants to approach and cuddle an infant belonging to another member of the troop. The young monkey is naturally rather frightened by the approach of the stranger and retreats. On such occasions it is possible to observe the large female attempting to reassure the tiny infant by making the lip-smacking face at it. If this calms the youngster's fears, the female can then fondle it and continue to calm it by gently grooming it.

Clearly, if we turn now to our own species, we might expect to see some manifestation of this basic primate grooming tendency, not only as a simple cleaning pattern, but also in a social context. The big difference, of course, is that we no longer have a luxuriant coat of fur to keep clean. When two naked apes meet and wish to reinforce their friendly relationship they must therefore find some kind of substitute for social grooming. If one studies those situations where, in another primate species, one would expect to see mutual grooming, it is intriguing to observe what happens. To start with it is obvious that smiling has replaced lip-smacking. Its origin as a special infantile signal has already been discussed and we have seen how, in the absence of the clinging response, it became necessary for the baby to have some way of attracting and pacifying the mother. Extended into adult life, the smile is clearly an excellent 'grooming-invitation' substitute. But, having invited friendly contact, what next? Somehow it has to be maintained. Lip-smacking is reinforced by grooming, but what reinforces smiling. True, the smiling response can be repeated and extended in time long after the initial contact, but something else is needed, something more 'occupational'. Some kind of activity, like grooming, has to be borrowed and converted. Simple observations reveal that the plundered source is verbalised vocalisation.

The behaviour pattern of talking evolved originally out of the increased need for the co-operative exchange of information. It grew out of the common and widespread animal phenomenon of non-verbal mood vocalisation. From the typical, inborn mammalian repertoire of grunts and squeals there developed a more complex series of learnt sound signals. These vocal units and their combinations and re-combinations became the basis of what we can call *information talking*. Unlike the more primitive non-verbal mood signals, this new method of communication enabled our ancestors to refer to objects in the environment and also to the past and the future as well as to the present. To this day, information talking has remained the most important form of vocal communication for our species. But, having evolved, it did not stop there. It acquired additional functions. One of these took the form of *mood talking*. Strictly speaking, this was unnecessary, because the non-verbal mood signals were not lost. We still can and do convey our emotional states by giving vent to ancient primate screams and grunts, but we augment these messages with verbal confirmation of our feelings. A yelp of pain is closely followed by a verbal signal that 'I am hurt'. A roar of anger is accompanied by the message 'I am furious'. Sometimes the non-verbal signal is not performed in its pure state but instead finds expression as a tone of voice. The words 'I am hurt' are whined or screamed. The words 'I am furious' are roared or bellowed. The tone of voice in such cases is so unmodified by learning and so close to the ancient non-verbal mammalian signalling system that even a dog can understand the message, let alone a foreigner from another race of our own species. The actual words used in such instances are almost superfluous. (Try snarling 'good dog', or cooing 'bad dog' at your pet, and you will see what I mean.) At its crudest and most intense level, mood talking is little more than a 'spilling over' of verbalised sound signalling into an area of communication that is already taken care of. Its value lies in the increased possibilities it provides for more subtle and sensitive mood signalling.

A third form of verbalisation is *exploratory talking*. This is talking for talking's sake, aesthetic talking, or, if you like, play talking. Just as that other form of information-transmission, picture-making, became used as a medium for aesthetic exploration, so did talking. The poet paralleled the painter. But it is the fourth type of verbalisation that we are concerned with in this chapter, the kind that has aptly been described recently as *grooming talking*. This is the meaningless, polite chatter of social occasions, the 'nice weather we are having' or 'have you read any good books lately' form of talking. It is not concerned with the exchange of important ideas or information, nor does it reveal the true mood of the speaker, nor is it aesthetically pleasing. Its function is to reinforce the greeting smile and to maintain the social togetherness. It is our substitute for social grooming. By providing us with a non-aggressive social preoccupation, it enables us to expose ourselves communally to one another over comparatively long periods, in this way enabling valuable group bonds and friendships to grow and become strengthened.

Viewed in this way, it is an amusing game to plot the course of grooming talk during a social encounter. It plays its most dominant role immediately after the initial greeting ritual. It then slowly loses ground, but has another peak of expression as the group breaks up. If the group has come together for purely social reasons, grooming talk may, of course, persist throughout to the complete exclusion of any kind of information, mood or exploratory talk. The cocktail party is a good example of this, and on such occasions 'serious' talking may even be actively suppressed by the host or hostess, who repeatedly intervene to break up long conversations and rotate the mutual-groomers to ensure maximum social contact. In this way, each member of the party is repeatedly thrown back into a state of 'initial contact', where the stimulus for grooming talk will be strongest. If these non-stop social grooming sessions are to be successful, a sufficiently large number of guests must be invited in order to prevent new contacts from running out before the party is over. This explains the mysterious minimum size that is always automatically recognised as essential for gatherings of this kind. Small, informal dinner parties provide a slightly different situation. Here the grooming talk can be observed to wane as the evening progresses and the verbal exchange of serious information and ideas can be seen to gain in dominance as time passes. Just before the party breaks up, however, there is a brief resurgence of grooming talk prior to the final parting ritual. Smiling also reappears at this point, and the social bonding is in this way given a final farewell boost to help carry it over to the next encounter.

If we switch our observations now to the more formal business encounter, where the prime function

179

of the contact is information talking, we can witness a further decline in the dominance of grooming talk, but not necessarily a total eclipse of it. Here its expression is almost entirely confined to the opening and closing moments. Instead of waning slowly, as at the dinner party, it is suppressed rapidly, after a few polite, initial exchanges. It reappears again, as before, in the closing moments of the meeting, once the anticipated moment of parting has been signalled in some way. Because of the strong urge to perform grooming talk, business groups are usually forced to heighten the formalisation of their meetings in some way, in order to suppress it. This explains the origin of committee procedure, where formality reaches a pitch rarely encountered on other private social occasions.

Although grooming talk is the most important substitute we have for social grooming, it is not our only outlet for this activity. Our naked skin may not send out very exciting grooming signals, but other more stimulating surfaces are frequently available and are used as substitutes. Fluffy or furry clothing, rugs, or furniture often release a strong grooming response. Pet animals are even more inviting, and few naked apes can resist the temptation to stroke a cat's fur, or scratch a dog behind the ear. The fact that the animal appreciates this social grooming activity provides only part of the reward for the groomer. More important is the outlet the pet animal's body surface gives us for our ancient primate grooming urges.

As far as our own bodies are concerned, we may be naked over most of our surfaces, but in the head region there is still a long and luxuriant growth of hair available for grooming. This receives a great deal of attention—far more than can be explained on a simple hygienic basis—at the hands of the specialist groomers, the barbers and hairdressers. It is not immediately obvious why mutual hairdressing has not become part of our ordinary domestic social gatherings. Why, for instance, have we developed grooming talk as our special substitute for the more typical primate friendship grooming, when we could so easily have concentrated our original grooming efforts in the head region? The explanation appears to lie in the sexual significance of the hair. In its present form the arrangement of the head hair differs strikingly between the two sexes and therefore provides a secondary sexual characteristic. Its sexual associations have inevitably led to its involvement in sexual behaviour patterns, so that stroking or manipulating the hair is now an action too heavily loaded with erotic significance to be permissible as a simple social friendship gesture. If, as a result of this, it is banned from communal gatherings of social acquaintances, it is necessary to find some other outlet for it. Grooming a cat or a sofa may provide an outlet for the urge to groom, but the need to *be* groomed requires a special context. The hairdressing salon is the perfect answer. Here the customer can indulge in the groomee role to his or her heart's content, without any fear of a sexual element creeping in to the proceedings. By making the professional groomers into a separate category, completely dissociated from the 'tribal' acquaintance-ship group, the dangers are eliminated. The use of male groomers for males and female groomers for females reduces the dangers still further. Where this is not done, the sexuality of the groomer is reduced in some way. If a female is attended by a male hairdresser, he usually behaves in an effeminate manner, regardless of his true sexual personality. Males are nearly always groomed by male barbers, but if a female masseuse is employed, she is typically rather masculine.

As a pattern of behaviour, hairdressing has three functions. It not only cleans the hair and provides an outlet for social grooming, but it also decorates the groomee. Decoration of the body for sexual, aggressive, or other social purposes is a widespread phenomenon in the case of the naked ape, and it has been discussed under other headings in other chapters. It has no real place in a chapter on comfort behaviour, except that it so often appears to grow out of some kind of grooming activity. Tattooing, shaving and plucking of hair, manicuring, ear-piercing and the more primitive forms of scarification all seem to have their origin in simple grooming actions. But, whereas grooming talk has been borrowed from elsewhere and utilised as a grooming substitute, here the reverse process has taken place and grooming actions have been borrowed and elaborated for other uses. In acquiring a display function, the original comfort actions concerned with skin care have been transformed into what amounts to skin mutilation.

This trend can also be observed in certain captive animals in a zoo. They groom and lick with abnormal intensity until they have plucked bare patches or inflicted small wounds, either on their own bodies or those of companions. Excessive grooming of this kind is caused by conditions of stress or boredom. Similar conditions may well have provoked members of our own species to mutilate their body surfaces, with the already exposed and hairless skin aiding and abetting the process. In our case, however, our inherent opportunism enabled us to exploit this otherwise dangerous and damaging tendency and press it into service as a decorative display device.

Another and more important trend has also developed out of simple skin care, and that is medical care. Other species have made little progress in this direction, but for the naked ape the growth of medical practice out of social grooming behaviour has had an enormous influence on the successful development of the species, especially in more recent times. In our closest relatives, the chimpanzees, we can already witness the beginning of this trend. In addition to the general skin care of mutual grooming, one chimpanzee has been seen to attend to the minor physical disabilities of another. Small sores or wounds are carefully examined and licked clean. Splinters are carefully removed by pinching the companion's skin between two forefingers. In one instance a female chimpanzee with a small cinder in her left eye was seen to approach a male, whimpering and obviously in distress. The male sat down and examined her intently and then proceeded to remove the cinder with great care and precision, gently using the tips of one finger from each hand. This is more than simple grooming. It is the first sign of true co-operative medical care. But for chimpanzees, the incident described is already the peak of expression. For our own species, with greatly increased intelligence and co-operativeness, specialised grooming of this kind was to be the starting point of a vast technology of mutual physical aid. The medical world today has reached a condition of such complexity that it has become, in social terms, the major expression of our animal comfort behaviour. From coping with minor discomforts it has expanded to deal with major diseases and gross bodily damage. As a biological phenomenon its achievements are unique, but in becoming rational, its irrational elements have been somewhat overlooked. In order to understand this, it is essential to distinguish between serious and trivial cases of 'indisposition'. As with any other species, a naked ape can break a leg or become infected with a vicious parasite on a purely accidental or chance basis. But in the case of trivial ailments, all is not what it seems. Minor infections and sicknesses are usually treated rationally, as if they are simply mild versions of serious illnesses, but there is strong evidence to suggest that they are in reality much more related to primitive 'grooming demands'. The medical symptoms reflect a behavioural problem that has taken a physical form, rather than a true physical problem.

Common examples of 'grooming invitation ailments', as we can call them, include coughs, colds, influenza, backache, headache, stomach upsets, skin rashes, sore throats, biliousness, tonsillitis and laryngitis. The condition of the sufferer is not serious, but sufficiently unhealthy to justify increased attention from social companions. The symptoms act in the same way as grooming invitation signals, releasing comfort behaviour from doctors, nurses, chemists, relations and friends. The groomee provokes friendly sympathy and care and this alone is usually enough to cure the illness. The administering of pills and medicines replaces the ancient grooming actions and provides an occupational ritual that sustains the groomee-groomer relationship through this special phase of social interaction. The exact nature of the chemicals prescribed is almost irrelevant and there is little difference at this level between the practices of modern medicine and those of ancient witch-doctoring.

The objection to this interpretation of minor ailments is likely to be based on the observation that real viruses or bacteria can be proved to be present. If they are there and can be shown to be the medical cause of the cold or stomach ache, then why should we seek for a behavioural explanation? The answer is that in any large city, for example, we are all exposed to these common viruses and bacteria all the time, but we only occasionally fall prey to them. Also, certain individuals are much more susceptible than others. Those members of a community who are either very successful or socially well adjusted rarely suffer from 'grooming invitation ailments'. Those that have temporary or long-standing social problems are, by contrast, highly susceptible. The most intriguing aspect of these ailments is the way they are tailored to the special demands of the individual. Supposing an actress, for example, is suffering from social tensions and strains, what happens? She loses her voice, develops laryngitis, so that she is forced to stop work and take a rest. She is comforted and looked after. The tension is resolved (for the time being, at least). If instead she had developed a skin rash on her body, her costume would have covered it and she could have gone on working. The tension would have continued. Compare her situation with that of an all-in wrestler. For him a loss of voice would be useless as a 'grooming invitation ailment', but a skin rash would be ideal, and it is precisely this ailment that wrestlers' doctors find is the muscle-men's most common complaint. In this connection it is amusing that one famous actress, whose reputation relies on her nude appearances in her films, suffers under stress not from laryngitis, but from skin rash. Because, like the wrestlers, her skin exposure is vital, she falls into their ailment category rather than into that of other actresses.

If the need for comfort is intense, then the ailment becomes more intense. The time in our lives when we receive the most elaborate care and protection is when we are infants in our cots. An ailment that is severe enough to put us helplessly to bed, therefore, has the great advantage of recreating for us all the comforting attention of our secure infancy. We may think we are taking a strong dose of medicine, but in reality

184

it is a strong dose of security that we need and that cures us. (This does not imply malingering. There is no need to malinger. The symptoms are real enough. It is the cause that is behavioural, not the effects.)

We are all to some extent frustrated groomers, as well as groomees, and the satisfaction that can be obtained from caring for the sick is as basic as the cause of the sickness. Some individuals have such a great need to care for others that they may actively promote and prolong sickness in a companion in order to be able to express their grooming urges more fully. This can produce a vicious circle, with the groomer-groomee situation becoming exaggerated out of all proportion, to the extent where a chronic invalid demanding (and getting) constant attention is created. If a 'mutual grooming pair' of this type were faced with the behavioural truth concerning their reciprocal conduct, they would hotly deny it. Nevertheless, it is astonishing what miraculous cures can sometimes be worked in such instances when a major social upheaval occurs in the groomer-groomee (nurse-patient) environment that has been created. Faith-healers have occasionally exploited this situation with startling results, but unfortunately for them many of the cases they encounter have physical causes as well as physical effects. Also working against them is the fact that the physical effects of behaviourally produced 'grooming invitation ailments' can easily create irreversible body damage if sufficiently prolonged or intense. Once this has happened, serious, rational medical treatment is required.

Up to this point I have been concentrating on the social aspects of comfort behaviour in our species. As we have seen there have been great developments in that direction, but this has not excluded or replaced the simpler kinds of self-cleaning and self-comfort. Like other primates we still scratch ourselves, rub our eyes, pick our sores, and lick our wounds. We also share with them a strong tendency to sun-bathe. In addition we have added a number of specialised cultural patterns, the most common and widespread of which is washing with water. This is rare in other primates, although certain species bathe occasionally, but for us it now plays the major role in body cleaning in most communities.

Despite its obvious advantages, frequent cleansing with water nevertheless puts a severe strain on the production of antiseptic and protective oils and salts by the skin glands, and to some extent it is bound to make the body surface more susceptible to diseases. It survives this disadvantage only because, at the same time that it eliminates the natural oils and salts, it removes the dirt that is the source of these diseases.

In addition to problems of keeping clean, the general category of comfort behaviour also includes those patterns of activity concerned with the task of maintaining a suitable body temperature. Like all mammals and birds, we have evolved a constant, high body temperature, giving us greatly increased physiological efficiency. If we are healthy, our deep body temperature varies no more than $3°$ Fahrenheit, regardless of the outside temperature. This internal temperature fluctuates with a daily rhythm, the highest level occurring in the late afternoon and the lowest at around 4 a.m. If the external environment becomes too hot or too cold we quickly experience acute discomfort. The unpleasant sensations we receive act as an early warning system, alerting us to the urgent need to take action to prevent the internal body organs from becoming disastrously chilled or overheated. In addition to encouraging intelligent, voluntary responses, the body also takes certain automatic steps to stabilise its heat level. If the environment becomes too hot, vasodilation occurs. This gives a hotter body surface and encourages heat loss from the skin. Profuse sweating also takes place. We each possess approximately two million sweat glands. Under conditions of intense heat these are capable of secreting a maximum of one litre of sweat per hour. The evaporation of this liquid from the body surface provides another valuable form of heat loss. During the process of acclimatisation to a generally hotter environment, we undergo a marked increase in sweating efficiency. This is vitally important because, even in the hottest climates, our internal body temperature can only stand an upward shift of $0.4°$ Fahrenheit, regardless our racial origin.

If the environment becomes too cold, we respond with vasoconstriction and with shivering. The vaso-constriction helps to conserve the body heat and the shivering can provide up to three times the resting heat production. If the skin is exposed to the intense cold for any length of time, there is a danger that the prolonged vasoconstriction will lead to frostbite. In the hand region there is an important, built-in, anti-frost-bite system. The hands at first respond to intense cold by drastic vasoconstriction; then, after about five minutes, this is reversed and there is strong vasodila-tion, the hands becoming hot and flushed. (Anyone who has been snowballing in winter will have experi-enced this.) The constriction and dilation of the hand region then continues to alternate, the constriction phases curtailing heat loss and the dilation phases preventing frostbite. Individuals living permanently in a cold climate undergo various forms of bodily acclimitisation, including a slightly increased basal metabolic rate.

As our species has spread over the globe, important cultural additions have been made to these biological temperature control mechanisms. The development of fire, clothing, and insulated dwelling-houses have com-bated heat loss, and ventilation and refrigeration have been used against heat gain. Impressive and dramatic as these advances have been, they have in no way altered our internal body temperature. They have merely served to control the external temperature, so that we can continue to enjoy our primitive primate temperature level in a more diverse range of external conditions. Despite recent claims, suspended animation experiments involving special freezing techniques are still confined to the realms of science fiction.

Before leaving the subject of temperature responses, there is one particular aspect of sweating that should be mentioned. Detailed studies of sweating responses in our species have revealed that they are not as simple as they may first appear. Most areas of the body sur-face begin to perspire freely under conditions of in-creased heat, and this is undoubtedly the original, basic response of the sweat-gland system. But certain regions have become reactive to other types of stimulation and sweating can occur there regardless of the external temperature. The eating of highly spiced foods, for example, produces its own special pattern of facial sweating. Emotional stress quickly leads to sweating on the palms of the hands, the soles of the feet, the armpits and sometimes also the forehead, but not on other parts of the body. There is a further distinction in the areas of emotional sweating, the palms and the soles differing from the armpits and the forehead. The first two regions respond well *only* to emotional situations, whereas the last two react to both emotional and to temperature stimuli. It is clear from this that the hands and feet have 'borrowed' sweating from the temperature control system and are now using it in a new functional context. The moistening of the palms and soles during stress appears to have become a special feature of the 'ready for anything' response that the body gives when danger threatens. Spitting on the hands before wielding an axe is, in a sense, the non-physiological equivalent of this process.

So sensitive is the palmar sweating response that whole communities or nations may show sudden increases in this reaction if their group security is threatened in some way. During a recent political crisis, when there was a temporary increase in the likelihood of nuclear war, all experiments into palmar sweating at a research institute had to be abandoned because the base level of the response had become so abnormal that the tests would have been meaningless. Having our palms read by a fortune-teller may not tell us much about the future, but having them read by a physiologist can certainly tell us something about our fears for the future.

CHAPTER EIGHT

ANIMALS

UP to this point we have been considering the naked ape's behaviour towards himself and towards members of his own species—his intra-specific behaviour. It now remains to examine his activities in relation to other animals—his inter-specific behaviour.

All the higher forms of animal life are aware of at least some of the other species with which they share their environment. They regard them in one of five ways: as prey, symbionts, competitors, parasites, or predators. In the case of our own species, these five categories may be lumped together as the 'economic' approach to animals, to which may be added the scientific, aesthetic and symbolic approaches. This wide range of interests has given us an inter-specific involvement unique in the animal world. In order to unravel it and understand it objectively we must tackle it step by step, attitude by attitude.

Because of his exploratory and opportunist nature, the naked ape's list of prey species is immense. At some place, at some time, he has killed and eaten almost any animal you care to mention. From a study of prehistoric remains we know that about half a million years ago, at one site alone, he was hunting and eating species of bison, horse, rhino, deer, bear, sheep, mammoth, camel, ostrich, antelope, buffalo, boar and hyaena. It would be pointless to compile a 'species menu' for more recent times but one feature of our predatory behaviour does deserve mention, namely our tendency to domesticate certain selected prey species. For, although we are likely to eat almost anything palatable on occasion, we have nevertheless limited the bulk of our feeding to a few major animal forms.

Domestication of livestock, involving the organised control and selective breeding of prey, is known to have been practised for at least ten thousand years and, in certain cases, probably much longer. Goats, sheep and reindeer appear to have been the earliest prey species dealt with in this way. Then, with the development of settled agricultural communities, pigs and cattle, including Asiatic buffalo and yak, were added to the list. We have evidence that, in the case of cattle, several distinct breeds had already been developed four thousand years ago. Whereas the goats, sheep and reindeer were transformed directly from hunted prey to herded prey, it is thought that the pigs and cattle began their close association with our species as crop-robbers. As soon as cultivated crops were available, they moved in to take advantage of this rich new food supply, only to be taken over by the early farmers and brought under domestic control themselves.

The only small mammalian prey species to undergo prolonged domestication was the rabbit, but this was apparently a much later development. Amongst the birds, important prey species domesticated thousands of years ago were the chicken, the goose and the duck, with later minor additions of the pheasant, guinea fowl, quail and turkey. The only prey fish with a long history of domestication are the Roman eel, the carp and the goldfish. The latter, however, soon became ornamental rather than gastronomic. The domestication of these fish is limited to the last two thousand years and has played only a small role in the general story of our organised predation.

The second category in our list of inter-specific relationships is that of the symbiont. Symbiosis is defined as the association of two different species to their mutual benefit. Many examples of this are known from the animal world, the most famous being the partnership between the tick birds and certain large ungulates such as the rhinoceros, giraffe and buffalo. The birds eat the skin parasites of the ungulates, helping to keep the bigger animals healthy and clean, while the latter provide the birds with a valuable source of food.

Where we ourselves are one of the members of a symbiotic pair, the mutual benefit tends to become biased rather heavily in our favour, but it is nevertheless a separate category, distinct from the more severe prey-predator relationship, since it does not involve the death of the other species concerned. They are exploited, but in exchange for the exploitation we feed and care for them. It is a biased symbiosis because we are in control of the situation and our animal partners usually have little or no choice in the matter.

The most ancient symbiont in our history is undoubtedly the dog. We cannot be certain exactly when our ancestors first began to domesticate this valuable animal, but it appears to be at least ten thousand years ago. The story is a fascinating one. The wild, wolf-like ancestors of the domestic dog must have been serious competitors with our hunting forebears. Both were co-operative pack-hunters of large prey and, at first, little love can have been lost between them. But the wild dogs possessed certain special refinements that our own hunters lacked. They were particularly adept at herding and driving prey during hunting man-oeuvres and could carry this out at high speed. They also had more delicate senses of smell and hearing. If these attributes could be exploited in exchange for a share in the kill, then the bargain was a good one. Somehow—we do not know exactly how—this came about and an interspecific bond was forged. It is probable that it began as a result of young puppies being brought in to the tribal home base to be fattened as food. The value of these creatures as alert nocturnal watch-dogs would have scored a mark in their favour at an early stage. Those that were allowed to live in a now tamed condition and permitted to accompany the males on their hunting trips would soon show their paces in assisting to track down the prey. Having been hand-reared, the dogs would consider themselves to be members of the naked-ape pack and would co-operate instinctively with their adopted leaders. Selective breeding over a number of generations would soon weed out the trouble-makers and a new, improved stock of increasingly restrained and controllable domestic hunting dogs would arise.

It has been suggested that it was this progression in the dog relationship that made possible the earliest forms of ungulate prey domestication. The goats, sheep and reindeer were under some degree of control before the advent of the true agricultural phase, and the improved dog is envisaged as the vital agent that made this feasible by assisting in the large-scale and long-term herding of these animals. Studies of the driving behaviour of present-day sheepdogs and of wild wolves reveal many similarities in technique and provide strong support for this view.

During more recent times, intensified selective breeding has produced a whole range of symbiotic dog specialisations. The primitive all-purpose hunting dog assisted in all stages of the operation, but his later descendants were perfected for one or other of the different components of the overall behaviour sequence. Individual dogs with unusually well-developed abilities in a particular direction were inbred to intensify their special advantages. As we have already seen, those with good qualities in manoeuvring became herding dogs, their contribution being confined largely to the rounding up of domesticated prey (sheepdogs). Others, with a superior sense of smell were inbred as scent-trackers (hounds). Others, with an athletic turn of speed, became coursing dogs and were employed to chase after prey by sight (greyhounds). Another group were bred as prey-spotters, their tendency to 'freeze' when locating the prey being exploited and intensified (setters and pointers). Yet another line was improved as prey-finders and carriers (retrievers). Small breeds were developed as vermin-killers (terriers). The primitive watchdogs were genetically improved as guard-dogs (mastiffs).

In addition to these widespread forms of exploitation, other dog lines have been selectively bred for more unusual functions. The most extraordinary example is the hairless dog of the ancient New World Indians, a genetically naked breed with an abnormally high skin temperature that was used as a primitive form of hot water-bottle in their sleeping quarters.

In more recent times, the symbiotic dog has earned his keep as beast of burden, pulling sledges or carts, as a messenger or a mine-detector during times of war, as a rescue operator, locating climbers buried under snow, as a police dog, tracking or attacking criminals, as a guide dog, leading the blind, and even as a substitute space-traveller. No other symbiotic species has served us in such a complex and varied way. Even today, with all our technological advances, the dog is still actively employed in most of his functional roles. Many of the hundreds of breeds that can now be distinguished are purely ornamental, but the day of the dog with a serious task to perform is far from over.

So successful has the dog been as a hunting companion that few attempts have been made to domesticate other species in this particular form of symbiosis. The only important exceptions are the cheetah and certain birds of prey, especially the falcon, but in neither case has any progress been made with regard to controlled breeding, let alone selective breeding. Individual training has always been required. In Asia the cormorant, a diving bird, has been used as an active companion in the hunt for fish. Cormorant eggs are taken and hatched out under domestic chickens. The young sea-birds are then hand-reared and trained to catch fish on the end of a line. The fish are brought back to the boats and disgorged, the cormorants having been fitted with a collar to prevent them swallowing their prey. But here again no attempt has been made to improve the stock by selective breeding.

Another ancient form of exploitation involves the use of small carnivores as pest-destroyers. This trend did not gain momentum until the agricultural phase of our history. With the development of large-scale grain storage, rodents became a serious problem and rodent-killers were encouraged. The cat, the ferret and the mongoose were the species that came to our aid and in the first two cases full domestication with selective breeding followed.

Perhaps the most important kind of symbiosis has been the utilisation of certain larger species as beasts of burden. Horses, onagers (Asiatic wild asses), donkeys (African wild asses), cattle, including the water buffalo and the yak, reindeer, camels, llamas and elephants have all been subjected to massive exploitation in this way. In most of these cases the original wild types have been 'improved' by careful selective breeding, the exceptions to this rule being the onager and the elephant. The onager was being used as a beast of burden by the ancient Sumerians over four thousand years ago, but was rendered obsolete by the introduction of a more easily controlled species, the horse. The elephant, although still employed as a working animal, has always offered too big a challenge to the stock-breeder and has never been submitted to the pressures of selective breeding.

A further category concerns the domestication of a variety of species as sources of produce. The animals are not killed, so that in this role they cannot be considered as prey. Only certain parts are taken from them: milk from cattle and goats, wool from sheep and alpaca, eggs from chickens and ducks, honey from bees and silk from silk-moths.

In addition to these major categories of hunting companions, pest-destroyers, beasts of burden, and sources of produce, certain animals have entered a symbiotic relationship with our species on a more unusual and specialised basis. The pigeon has been domesticated as a message-carrier. The astonishing homing abilities of this bird have been exploited for thousands of years. This relationship became so valuable in times of war that, during recent epochs, a counter-symbiosis was developed in the form of falcons trained to intercept the message-carriers. In a very different context, Siamese fighting fish and fighting cocks have been selectively bred over a long period as gambling devices. In the realm of medicine, the guinea-pig and the white rat have been widely employed as 'living test-beds' for laboratory experiments.

These, then, are the major symbionts, animals that have been forced into some form of partnership with our ingenious species. The advantage to them is that they cease to be our enemies. Their numbers are dramatically increased. In terms of world populations they are tremendously successful. But it is a qualified success. The price they have paid is their evolutionary freedom. They have lost their genetic independence and, although well fed and cared for, are now subject to our breeding whims and fancies.

The third major category of animal relationships, after prey and symbionts, is that of competitors. Any species which competes with us for food or space, or interferes with the efficient running of our lives, is ruthlessly eliminated. There is no point in listing such species. Virtually any animal that is either inedible or symbiotically useless is attacked and exterminated. This process is continuing today in all parts of the world. In the case of minor competitors, the persecution is haphazard, but serious rivals stand little chance. In the past our closest primate relatives have been our most threatening rivals and it is no accident that today we are the only species surviving in our entire family. Large carnivores have been our other serious competitors and these too have been eliminated wherever the population density of our species has risen above a certain level. Europe, for example, is now virtually denuded of all large forms of animal life, save for a great seething mass of naked apes.

For the next major category, that of parasites, the future looks even more bleak. Here the fight is intensified and although we may mourn the passing of an attractive food rival, no one will shed a tear over the increasing rarity of the flea. As medical science progresses, the grip of the parasites dwindles. In its wake this brings an added threat to all the other species, for as the parasites go and our health increases, our populations can swell at an even more startling rate, thus accentuating the need to eliminate all the milder competitors.

The fifth major category, the predators, are also on the way out. We have never really constituted a main diet component for any species, and our numbers have never been seriously reduced by predation at any stage in our history, as far as we can tell. But the larger carnivores, such as the big cats and the wild dogs, the bigger members of the crocodile family, the sharks and the more massive birds of prey have nibbled away at us from time to time and their days are clearly numbered. Ironically, the killer that has accounted for more naked-ape deaths than any other (parasites excepted) is one that cannot devour the nutritious corpses it produces. This deadly enemy is the venemous snake and, as we shall see later, this has become the most hated of all higher forms of animal life.

These five categories of inter-specific relationships—

prey, symbiont, competitor, parasite and predator—
are the ones that can be found to exist between other
pairs of species. Basically, we are not unique in these
respects. We carry the relationships much further than
other species, but they are the same types of relationships. As I said earlier, they can be lumped together
as the economic approach to animals. In addition we
have our own special approaches, the scientific, the
aesthetic and the symbolic.

The scientific and aesthetic attitudes are manifestations of our powerful exploratory drive. Our curiosity,
our inquisitiveness, urges us on to investigate all
natural phenomena and the animal world has naturally been the focus of much attention in this respect.
To the zoologist, all animals are, or should be, equally
interesting. To him there are no bad species or good
species. He studies them all, exploring them for their
own sake. The aesthetic approach involves the same
basic exploration, but with different terms of reference. Here, the enormous variety of animal shapes,
colours, patterns and movements are studied as objects
of beauty rather than as systems for analysis.

The symbolic approach is entirely different. In this
case, neither economics nor exploration are involved.
The animals are employed instead as personifications
of concepts. If a species looks fierce, it becomes a war-
symbol. If it looks clumsy and cuddly, it becomes a
child-symbol. Whether it is genuinely fierce or genuinely cuddly, matters little. Its true nature is not in-
vestigated in this context, for this is not a scientific
approach. The cuddly animal may be bristling with
razor-sharp teeth and be endowed with a vicious
aggressiveness, but providing these attributes are not
obvious and its cuddliness is, it is perfectly acceptable
as the ideal child-symbol. For the symbolic animal,
justice does not have to be done, it has only to appear
to be done.

The symbolic attitude to animals was originally
christened the 'anthropoidomorphic' approach. Merci-
fully, this ugly term was later contracted to 'anthropomorphic' which, although still clumsy, is the
expression in general use today. It is invariably used
in a derogatory sense by scientists who, from their

point of view, are fully justified in scorning it. They must retain their objectivity at all costs if they are to make meaningful explorations into the animal world. But this is not as easy as it may sound.

Quite apart from deliberate decisions to use animal forms as idols, images and emblems, there are also subtle, hidden pressures working on us all the time that force us to see other species as caricatures of ourselves. Even the most sophisticated scientist is liable to say, 'Hallo, old boy' when greeting his dog. Although he knows perfectly well that the animal cannot understand his words, he cannot resist the temptation. What is the nature of these anthropomorphic pressures and why are they so difficult to overcome? Why do some creatures make us say 'Aah' and others make us say 'Ugh!'? This is no trivial consideration. A vast amount of our present culture's inter-specific energies are involved here. We are passionate animal lovers and animal haters, and these involvements cannot be explained on the basis of economic and exploratory considerations alone. Clearly some kind of unsuspected, basic response is being triggered off inside us by the specific signals we are receiving. We delude ourselves that we are responding to the animal as an animal. We declare that is it charming, irresistible, or horrible, but what makes it so?

In order to find the answer to this question we must first assemble some facts. What exactly are the animal loves and animal hates of our culture and how do they vary with age and sex? Quantitative evidence is required on a large scale if reliable statements are to be made on this topic. To obtain such evidence an investigation was carried out involving 80,000 British children between the ages of four and fourteen. During a zoo television programme they were asked the simple question: 'Which animal do you like most?' and 'Which animal do you dislike most?' From the massive response to this inquiry a sample of 12,000 replies to each question was selected at random and analysed.

Dealing first with the interspecific 'loves', how did the various groups of animals fare? The figures are as follows: 97.15 per cent of all the children quoted a mammal of some kind as their top favourite. Birds accounted for only 1.6 per cent, reptiles 1.0 per cent, fish 0.1 per cent, invertebrates 0.1 per cent, and amphibians 0.05 per cent. Obviously there is something special about mammals in this context.

(It should perhaps be pointed out that the replies to the questions were written, not spoken, and it was sometimes difficult to identify the animals from the names given, especially in the case of very young children. It was easy enough to decipher loins, hores, bores, penny kings, panders, tapers and leapolds, but almost impossible to be certain of the species referred to as bettle twigs, the skipping worm, the otamus, or the coco-cola beast. Entries supporting these appealing creatures were reluctantly rejected.)

If we now narrow our sights to the 'top ten animal loves' the figures emerge as follows: 1. Chimpanzee (13.5 per cent). 2. Monkey (13 per cent). 3. Horse (9 per cent). 4. Bushbaby (8 per cent). 5. Panda (7.5 per cent). 6. Bear (7 per cent). 7. Elephant (6 per cent). 8. Lion (5 per cent). 9. Dog (4 per cent). 10. Giraffe (2.5 per cent).

It is immediately clear that these preferences do not reflect powerful economic or aesthetic influences. A list of the ten most important economic species would read very differently. Nor are these animal favourites the most elegant and brightly coloured of species. They include instead a high proportion of rather clumsy, heavy-set and dully coloured forms. They are, however, well endowed with anthropomorphic features and it is to these that the children are responding when making their choices. This is not a conscious process. Each of the species listed provides certain key stimuli strongly reminiscent of special properties of our own species, and to these we react automatically without any realisation of what it is exactly that appeals to us. The most significant of these anthropomorphic features in the top ten animals are as follows:

1. They all have hair, rather than feathers or scales. 2. They have rounded outlines (chimpanzee, monkey, bushbaby, panda, bear elephant). 3. They have flat faces (chimpanzee, monkey, bushbaby, bear, panda, lion). 4. They have facial expressions (chimpanzee, monkey, horse, lion, dog). 5. They can 'manipulate'

small objects (chimpanzee, monkey, bushbaby, panda, elephant). 6. Their postures are in some ways, or at some times, rather vertical (chimpanzee, monkey, bushbaby, panda, bear, giraffe).

The more of these points a species can score, the higher up the top ten list it comes. Non-mammalian species fare badly because they are weak in these respects. Amongst the birds, the top favourites are the penguin (0·8 per cent) and the parrot (0·2 per cent). The penguin achieves the number one avian position because it is the most vertical of all the birds. The parrot also sits more vertically on its perch than most birds and it has several other special advantages. Its beak shape gives it an unusually flattened face for a bird. It also feeds in a strange way, bringing its foot up to its mouth rather than lowering its head, and it can mimic our vocalisations. Unfortunately for its popularity, it lowers itself into a more horizontal posture when walking and in this way loses points heavily to the vertically waddling penguin.

Amongst the top mammals there are several special points worth noting. Why, for instance, is the lion the only one of the big cats to be included? The answer appears to be that it alone, in the male, has a heavy mane of hair surrounding the head region. This has the effect of flattening the face (as is clear from the way lions are portrayed in children's drawings) and helps to score extra points for this species.

Facial expressions are particularly important, as we have already seen in earlier chapters, as basic forms of visual communication in our species. They have evolved in a complex form in only a few groups of mammals—the higher primates, the horses, the dogs and the cats. It is no accident that five of the top ten favourites belong to these groups. Changes in facial expression indicate changes in mood and this provides a valuable link between the animal and ourselves, even though the correct significance of the expressions is not always precisely understood.

As regards manipulative ability, the panda and the elephant are unique cases. The former has evolved an elongated wrist bone with which it can grasp the thin bamboo sticks on which it feeds. A structure of this kind is found nowhere else in the animal kingdom. It gives the flat-footed panda the ability to hold small objects and bring them up to its mouth while sitting in a vertical posture. Anthropomorphically this scores heavily in its favour. The elephant is also capable of 'manipulating' small objects with its trunk, another unique structure, and taking them up to its mouth.

The vertical posture so characteristic of our species gives any other animal that can adopt this position an immediate anthropomorphic advantage. The primates in the top ten list, the bears and the panda all sit up vertically on frequent occasions. Sometimes they may even stand vertically or go so far as to take a few faltering steps in this position, all of which helps them to score valuable points. The giraffe, by virtue of its unique body proportions, is, in a sense, permanently vertical. The dog, which achieves such a high anthropomorphic score for its social behaviour, has always been something of a postural disappointment. It is uncompromisingly horizontal. Refusing to accept defeat on this point, our ingenuity went to work and soon solved the problem—we taught the dog to sit up and beg. In our urge to anthropomorphise the poor creature, we went further still. Being tailless ourselves, we started docking its tail. Being flat-faced ourselves, we employed selective breeding to reduce the bone structure in the snout region. As a result, many dog breeds are now abnormally flat-faced. Our anthropomorphic desires are so demanding that they have to be satisfied, even at the expense of the animals' dental efficiency. But then we must recall that this approach to animals is a purely selfish one. We are not seeing animals as animals, but merely as reflections of ourselves, and if the mirror distorts too badly we either bend it into shape or discard it.

So far we have been considering the animal loves of children of all ages between four and fourteen. If we now split up the responses to these favourite animals, separating them into age groups, some remarkably consistent trends emerge. For certain of the animals there is a steady decrease in preference with the increasing age of the children. For others there is a steady rise.

The unexpected discovery here is that these trends show a marked relationship with one particular feature of the preferred animals, namely their body size. The younger children prefer the bigger animals and the older children prefer the smaller ones. To illustrate this we can take the figures for the two largest of the top ten forms, the elephant and the giraffe, and two of the smallest, the bushbaby and the dog. The elephant, with an overall average rating of 6 per cent, starts out at 15 per cent with the four-year-olds and then falls smoothly to 3 per cent with the fourteen-year-olds. The giraffe shows a similar drop in popularity from 10 per cent to 1 per cent. The bushbaby, on the other hand, starts at only 4·5 per cent with the four-year-olds and then rises gradually to 11 per cent with the fourteen-year-olds. The dog rises from 0·5 to 6·5 per cent. The medium-sized animals amongst the top ten favourites do not show these marked trends.

We can sum up the findings so far by formulating two principles. The first law of animal appeal states that 'The popularity of an animal is directly correlated with the number of anthropomorphic features it possesses.' The second law of animal appeal states that 'The age of a child is inversely correlated with the size of the animal it most prefers.'

How can we explain the second law? Remembering that the preference is based on a symbolic equation, the simplest explanation is that the smaller children are viewing the animals as parent-substitutes and the older children are looking upon them as child-substitutes. It is not enough that the animal must remind us of our own species, it must remind us of a special category within it. When the child is very young, its parents are all-important protective figures. They dominate the child's awareness. They are large, friendly animals, and large friendly animals are therefore easily identified with parental figures. As the child grows it starts to assert itself, to compete with its parents. It sees itself in control of the situation, but it is difficult to control an elephant or a giraffe. The preferred animal has to shrink down to a manageable size. The child, in a strangely precocious way, becomes the parent itself. The animal has become the symbol of *its* child. The real child is too young to be a real parent, so instead it becomes a symbolic parent. Ownership of the animal becomes important and pet-keeping develops as a form of 'infantile parentalism'. It is no accident that, since becoming available as an exotic pet, the animal previously known as the galago has now acquired the popular name of bush*baby*. (Parents should be warned from this that the pet-keeping urge does not arrive until late in childhood. It is a grave error to provide pets for very young children, who respond to them as objects for destructive exploration, or as pests.)

There is one striking exception to the second law of animal appeal and that concerns the horse. The response to this animal is unusual in two ways. When analysed against increase in age of children, it shows a smooth rise in popularity followed by an equally smooth fall. The peak coincides with the onset of puberty. When analysed against the different sexes, it emerges that it is three times as popular with girls as with boys. No other animal love shows anything approaching this sex difference. Clearly there is something unusual about the response to the horse and it requires separate consideration.

The unique feature of the horse in the present context is that it is something to be mounted and ridden. This applies to none of the other top ten animals. If we couple this observation with the facts that its popularity peak coincides with puberty and that there is a strong sexual difference in its appeal, we are forced to the conclusion that the response to the horse must involve a strong sexual element. If a symbolic equation is being made between mounting a horse and sexual mounting, then it is perhaps surprising that the animal has a greater appeal for girls. But the horse is a powerful, muscular and dominant animal and is therefore more suited to the male role. Viewed objectively, the act of horse-riding consists of a long series of rhythmic movements with the legs wide apart and in close contact with the body of the animal. Its appeal for girls appears to result from the combination of its masculinity and the nature of the posture and actions performed on its back. It must be stressed here that we are dealing with the child population as a whole. One child in every eleven preferred the horse to all other animals. Only a small fraction of this percentage would ever actually own a pony or a horse. Those that do, quickly learn the many more varied rewards that go with this activity. If, as a result, they become addicted to horse-riding, this is not, of course, necessarily significant in the context we have been discussing.)

It remains to explain the fall in popularity of the horse following puberty. With increasing sexual development, it might be expected to show further increases in popularity, rather than a decrease. The answer can be found by comparing the graph for horse love with the curve for sex play in children. They match one another remarkably well. It would seem that, with the growth of sexual awareness, and the characteristic sense of privacy that comes to surround teenage sexual feelings, the response to the horse declines along with the decline in overt sex-play 'romping'. It is significant here that the appeal of monkeys also suffers a decline at this point. Many monkeys have particularly obtrusive sexual organs, including large, pink, sexual swellings. For the younger child these have no significance and the monkeys' other powerful anthropomorphic features can operate unhindered. But for older children the conspicuous genitals become a source of embarrassment and the popularity of these animals suffers as a consequence.

This, then, is the situation with regard to animal 'loves' in children. For adults, the responses become more varied and sophisticated, but the basic anthropomorphism persists. Serious naturalists and zoologists bewail this fact, but providing it is fully realised that symbolic responses of this kind tell us nothing about the true nature of the different animals concerned, they do little harm and provide a valuable subsidiary outlet for emotional feelings.

Before considering the other side of the coin—the animal 'hates'—there is one criticism that must be answered. It could be argued that the results discussed above are of purely cultural significance, and have no meaning for our species as a whole. As regards the exact identity of the animals involved this is true. To respond to a panda, it is obviously necessary to learn of its existence. There is no inborn panda response. But this is not the point. The choice of the panda may be culturally determined, but the *reasons* for choosing it do reflect a deeper, more biological process at work. If the investigation were repeated in another culture, the favourite species might be different, but they would still be selected according to our fundamental symbolic needs. The first and second law of animal appeal would still operate.

Turning now to animal 'hates', we can subject the figures to a similar analysis. The top ten most disliked animals are as follows: 1. Snake (27 per cent). 2. Spider (9.5 per cent). 3. Crocodile (4.5 per cent). 4. Lion (4.5 per cent). 5. Rat (4 per cent). 6. Skunk (3 per cent). 7. Gorilla (3 per cent). 8. Rhinoceros (3 per cent). 9. Hippopotamus (2.5 per cent). 10. Tiger (2.5 per cent).

These animals share one important feature: they are dangerous. The crocodile, the lion and the tiger are carnivorous killers. The gorilla, the rhinoceros and the hippopotamus can easily kill if provoked. The skunk indulges in a violent form of chemical warfare. The rat is a pest that spreads disease. There are venomous snakes and poisonous spiders.

Most of these creatures are also markedly lacking in the anthropomorphic features that typify the top ten favourites. The lion and the gorilla are exceptions. The lion is the only form to appear in both the top ten lists. The ambivalence of the response to this species is due to this animal's unique combination of attractive anthropomorphic characters and violent predatory behaviour. The gorilla is strongly endowed with anthropomorphic characters, but unfortunately for him his facial structure is such that he appears to be in a constantly aggressive and fearsome mood. This is merely an accidental outcome of his bone structure and bears no relationship to his true (and rather gentle) personality, but combined with his great physical strength it immediately converts him into a perfect symbol of savage brute force.

The most striking feature of the list of top ten hates is the massive response to the snake and the spider.

This cannot be explained solely on the basis of the existence of dangerous species. Other forces are at work. An analysis of the reasons given for hating these forms reveals that snakes are disliked because they are 'slimy and dirty' and spiders are repulsive because they are 'hairy and creepy'. This must mean either that they have a strong symbolic significance of some kind, or alternatively that we have a powerful inborn response to avoid these animals.

The snake has long been thought of as a phallic symbol. Being a poisonous phallus, it has represented unwelcome sex, which may be a partial explanation for its unpopularity; but there is more to it than this. If we examine the different levels of snake hatred in children between the ages of four and fourteen, it emerges that the peak of unpopularity comes early, long before puberty is reached. Even at four, the hate level is high—around 30 per cent—and it then climbs slightly, reaching its peak at age six. From then on it shows a smooth decline, sinking to well below 20 per cent by the age of fourteen. There is little difference between the sexes, although at each age level the response from girls is slightly stronger than the response from boys. The arrival of puberty appears to have no impact on the response in either sex.

From this evidence it is difficult to accept the snake simply as a strong sexual symbol. It seems more likely that we are dealing here with an inborn aversion response of our species towards snake-like forms. This would explain not only the early maturation of the reaction, but also the enormously high level of the response when compared with all other animal hates and loves. It would also fit with what we know of our closest living relatives, the chimpanzees, gorillas and orangutans. These animals also exhibit a great fear of snakes and here again it matures early. It is not seen in the very young apes, but is fully developed by the time they are a few years old and have reached the stage where they are beginning to make brief sorties away from the security of their mothers' bodies. For them an aversion response clearly has an important survival value and would also have been a great benefit to our early ancestors. Despite this, it has been argued that the snake reaction is not inborn, but merely a cultural phenomenon resulting from individual learning. Young chimpanzees reared under abnormally isolated conditions have reputedly failed to show the fear response when first exposed to snakes. But these experiments are not very convincing. In some instances, the chimpanzees have been too young when first tested. Had they been re-tested a few years later, the reaction may well have been present. Alternatively, the effects of isolation may have been so severe that the young animals in question were virtually mental defectives. Such experiments are based on a fundameneal misconception about the nature of inborn responses, which do not mature in an encapsulated form, irrespective of the outside environment. They should be thought of more as inborn susceptibilities. In the case of the snake response, it may be necessary for the young chimpanzee, or child, to encounter a number of different frightening objects in its early life and to learn to respond negatively to these. The inborn element in the snake case would then manifest itself in the form of a much more massive response to this stimulus than to others. The snake fear would be out of all proportion to the other fears, and this disproportionateness would be the inborn factor. The terror produced in normal young chimpanzees by exposure to a snake and the intense hatred of snakes exhibited by our own species is difficult to explain in any other way.

The reaction of children to spiders takes a rather different course. Here there is a marked sex difference. In boys there is an increase in spider hatred from age four to fourteen, but it is slight. The level of the reaction is the same for girls up to the age of puberty, but it then shows a dramatic rise, so that by the age of fourteen it is double that of the boys. Here we do seem to be dealing with an important symbolic factor. In evolutionary terms, poisonous spiders are just as dangerous to males as to females. There may or may not be an inborn response to these creatures in both sexes, but it cannot explain the spectacular leap in spider hatred that accompanies female puberty. The only clue here is the repeated female reference to spiders being nasty, hairy things. Puberty is, of course, the stage when tufts of body hair are beginning to sprout on both boys and girls. To children, body hairiness must appear as an essentially masculine character. The growth of hair on the body of a young girl would therefore have a more disturbing (unconscious) significance for her than it would in the case of a boy. The long legs of a spider are more hairlike and more obvious than those of other small creatures such as flies, and it would as a result be the ideal symbol in this role.

These, then, are the loves and the hatreds we experience when encountering or contemplating other species. Combined with our economic, scientific and aesthetic interests, they add up to a uniquely complex inter-specific involvement, and one which changes as we grow older. We can sum this up by saying that there are 'seven ages' of inter-specific reactivity. The first age is the *infantile phase*, when we are completely dependent on our parents and react strongly to very big animals, employing them as parent symbols. The second is the *infantile-parental phase*, when we are beginning to compete with our parents and react strongly to small animals that we can use as child-substitutes. This is the age of pet-keeping. The third age is the *objective pre-adult phase*, the stage where the exploratory interests, both scientific and aesthetic, come to dominate the symbolic. It is the time for bug-hunting, microscopes, butterfly-collecting and aquaria. The fourth is the *young adult phase*. At this point the most important animals are members of the opposite sex of our own species. Other species lose ground here, except in a purely commercial or economic context. The fifth is the *adult parental phase*. Here symbolic animals enter our lives again, but this time as pets for our children. The sixth age is the *post-parental phase*, when we lose our children and may turn once more to animals as child-substitutes to replace them. (In the case of childless adults, the use of animals as child-substitutes may, of course, begin earlier.) Finally, we come to the seventh age, the *senile phase*, which is characterised by a heightened interest in animal preservation and conservation. At this point the interest is focused on those species which are in danger of extermination. It makes little difference whether, from other points of view, they are attractive or repulsive, useful or useless, providing their numbers are few and becoming fewer. The increasingly rare rhinoceros and gorilla, for example, that are so disliked by children, become the centre of attention at this stage. They have to be 'saved'. The symbolic equation involved here is obvious enough: the senile individual is about to become personally extinct and so employs rare animals as symbols of his own impending doom. His emotional concern to save them from extinction reflects his desire to extend his own survival.

During recent years, interest in animal conservation has spread to some extent into the lower age groups, apparently as a result of the development of immensely powerful nuclear weapons. Their huge destructive potential threatens all of us, regardless of age, with the possibility of immediate extermination, so that now we all have an emotional need for animals that can serve as rarity symbols.

This observation should not be interpreted as implying that this is the only reason for the conservation of wild life. There are, in addition, perfectly valid scientific and aesthetic reasons why we should wish to give aid to unsuccessful species. If we are to continue to enjoy the rich complexities of the animal world and to use wild animals as objects of scientific and aesthetic exploration, we must give them a helping hand. If we allow them to vanish, we shall have simplified our environment in a most unfortunate way. Being an intensely investigatory species, we can ill afford to lose such a valuable source of material.

Economic factors are also sometimes mentioned when conservation problems are under discussion. It is pointed out that intelligent protection and controlled cropping of wild species can assist the protein-starved populations in certain parts of the world. While this is perfectly true on a short-term basis, the long-term picture is more gloomy. If our numbers continue to increase at the present frightening rate, it will eventually become a matter of choosing between us and them. No matter how valuable they are to us symbolically, scientifically or aesthetically, the economics of the situation will shift against them. The blunt fact is that when our own species density reaches a certain pitch, there will be no space left for other animals. The argument that they constitute an essential source of food does not, unhappily, stand up to close scrutiny. It is more efficient to eat plant food direct, than to convert it into animal flesh and then eat the animals. As the demand for living space increases still further, even more drastic steps will ultimately have to be taken and we shall be driven to synthesising our foodstuffs. Unless we can colonise other planets on a massive scale and spread the load, or seriously check our population increase in some way, we shall, in the not-too-far distant future, have to remove all other forms of life from the earth.

If this sounds rather melodramatic, consider the figures involved. At the end of the seventeenth century the world population of naked apes was only 500 million. It has now risen to 3,000 million. Every twenty-four hours it increases by another 150,000. (The inter-planetary emigration authorities would find this figure a daunting challenge.) In 260 years' time, if the rate of increase stays steady—which is unlikely—there will be a seething mass of 400,000 million naked apes crowding the face of the earth. This gives a figure of 11,000 individuals to every square mile of the entire land surface. To put it another way, the densities we now experience in our major cities would exist in every corner of the globe. The consequence of this for all forms of wild life is obvious. The effect it would have on our own species is equally depressing.

We need not dwell on this nightmare: the possibility of its becoming a reality is remote. As I have stressed throughout this book, we are, despite all our great technological advances, still very much a simple biological phenomenon. Despite our grandiose ideas and our lofty self-conceits, we are still humble animals, subject to all the basic laws of animal behaviour. Long before our populations reach the levels envisaged above we shall have broken so many of the rules that govern our biological nature that we shall have collapsed as a dominant species. We tend to suffer from a strange complacency that this can never happen, that there is something special about us, that we are somehow above biological control. But we are not. Many exciting species have become extinct in the past and we are no exception. Sooner or later we shall go, and make way for something else. If it is to be later rather than sooner, then we must take a long, hard look at ourselves as biological specimens and gain some understanding of our limitations. This is why I have written this book, and why I have deliberately insulted us by referring to us as naked apes, rather than by the more usual name we use for ourselves. It helps to keep a sense of proportion and to force us to consider what is going on just below the surface of our lives. In my enthusiasm I may, perhaps, have over-stated my case. There are many praises I could have sung, many magnificent achievements I could have described. By omitting them I have inevitably given a one-sided picture. We are an extraordinary species and I do not wish to deny it, or to belittle us. But these things have been said so often. When the coin is tossed it always seems to come up heads, and I have felt that it was high time we turned it over and looked at the other side. Unfortunately, because we are so powerful and so successful when compared with other animals, we find the contemplation of our humble origins somehow offensive, so that I do not expect to be thanked for what I have done. Our climb to the top has been a get-rich-quick story, and, like all *nouveaux riches*, we are very sensitive about our background. We are also in constant danger of betraying it.

Optimism is expressed by some who feel that since we have evolved a high level of intelligence and a strong inventive urge, we shall be able to twist any situation to our advantage; that we are so flexible that we can re-mould our way of life to fit any of the new demands made by our rapidly rising species-status; that when the time comes, we shall manage to cope with the over-crowding, the stress, the loss of our privacy and independence of action; that we shall re-model our behaviour patterns and live like giant ants; that we shall control our aggressive and territorial feelings, our sexual impulses and our parental tendencies; that if we have to become battery chicken-apes, we can do it; that our intelligence can dominate all our basic biological urges. I submit that this is rubbish. Our raw animal nature will never permit it. Of course, we are flexible. Of course, we are behavioural opportunists, but there are severe limits to the form our opportunism can take. By stressing our biological features in this book, I have tried to show the nature of these restrictions. By recognising them clearly and submitting to them, we shall stand a much better chance of survival. This does not imply a naïve 'return to nature'. It simply means that we should tailor our intelligent opportunist advances to our basic behavioural requirements. We must somehow improve in quality rather than in sheer quantity. If we do this, we can continue to progress technologically in a dramatic and exciting way without denying our evolutionary inheritance. If we do not, then our suppressed biological urges will build up and up until the dam bursts and the whole of our elaborate existence is swept away in the flood.

APPENDIX: LITERATURE

It is impossible to list all the many works that have been of assistance in writing *The Naked Ape*, but some of the more important ones are arranged below on a chapter-by-chapter and topic-by-topic basis. Detailed references for these publications are given in the bibliography that follows this appendix.

Chapter One. Origins
Classification of primates: Morris, 1965. Napier and Napier, 1967.
Evolution of primates: Dart and Craig, 1959. Eimerl and DeVore, 1965. Hooton, 1947. Le Gros Clark, 1959. Morris and Morris, 1966. Napier and Napier, 1967. Oakley, 1961. Read, 1925. Washburn, 1962 and 1964. Tax, 1960.
Carnivore behaviour: Guggisberg, 1961. Kleiman, 1966. Kruuk, 1966. Leyhausen, 1956. Lorenz, 1954. Moulton, Ashton and Eayrs, 1960. Neuhaus, 1953. Young and Goldman, 1944.
Primate behaviour: Morris, 1967. Morris and Morris, 1966. Schaller, 1963. Southwick, 1963. Yerkes and Yerkes, 1929. Zuckerman, 1932.

Chapter Two. Sex
Animal courtship: Morris, 1956.
Sexual responses: Masters and Johnson, 1966.
Sexual pattern frequencies: Kinsey *et al.*, 1948 and 1953.
Self-mimicry: Wickler, 1963 and 1967.
Mating postures: Ford and Beach, 1952.
Odour preferences: Monicreff, 1965.
Chastity devices: Gould and Pyle, 1896.
Homosexuality: Morris, 1955.

Chapter Three. Rearing
Suckling: Gunther, 1955. Lipsitt, 1966.

Heart-beat response: Salk, 1966.
Growth rates: Harrison, Weiner, Tanner and Barnicott, 1964.
Sleep: Kleitman, 1963.
Stages of development: Shirley, 1933.
Development of vocabulary: Smith, 1926.
Chimpanzee vocal imitations: Hayes, 1952.
Crying, smiling and laughing: Ambrose, 1960.
Facial expressions in primates: van Hooff, 1962.
Group density in children: Hutt and Vaizey, 1966.

Chapter Four.   Exploration
Neophilia and neophobia: Morris, 1964.
Ape picture-making: Morris, 1962.
Infant picture-making: Kellogg, 1955.
Chimpanzee exploratory behaviour: Morris and Morris, 1966.
Isolation during infancy: Harlow, 1958.
Stereotyped behaviour: Morris, 1964 and 1966.

Chapter Five.   Aggression
Primate aggression: Morris and Morris, 1966.
Autonomic changes: Cannon, 1929.
Origin of signals: Morris, 1956 and 1957.
Displacement activities: Tinbergen, 1951.
Facial expressions: van Hooff, 1962.
Eye-spot signals: Coss, 1965.
Reddening of buttocks: Comfort, 1966.
Redirection of aggression: Bastock, Morris and Moynihan, 1953.
Over-crowding in animals: Calhoun, 1962.

Chaper Six.   Feeding
Male association patterns: Tiger, 1967.
Organs of taste and smell: Wyburn, Pickford and Hirst, 1964.
Cereal diets: Harrison, Weiner, Tanner and Barnicott, 1964.

Chapter Seven.   Comfort
Social grooming: van Hooff, 1962. Sparks, 1963 (I am particularly indebted to Jan van Hooff for inventing the term 'Grooming talk'.)

Skin glands: Montagna, 1956.
Temperature responses: Harrison, Weiner, Tanner and Barnicott, 1964.
'Medical' aid in chimpanzees: Miles, 1963.

  Chapter Eight.   Animals
Domestication: Zeuner, 1963.
Animal likes: Morris and Morris, 1966.
Animal dislikes: Morris and Morris, 1965.
Animal phobias: Marks, 1966.
Population explosion: Fremlin, 1965.

BIBLIOGRAPHY

AMBROSE, J. A., 'The smiling response in early human infancy' (Ph.D.thesis, London University, 1960), pp. 1-660.

BASTOCK, M., D. MORRIS, and M. MOYNIHAN, 'Some comments on conflict and thwarting in animals'. *Behaviour* 6 (1953), pp. 66-84.

BEACH, F. A. (editor), *Sex and Behaviour* (Wiley, New York, 1965).

BERELSON, B. and G. A. STEINER, *Human Behaviour* (Harcourt, Brace and World, New York, 1964).

CALHOUN, J. B., 'A "behavioral sink",' in *Roots of Behaviour*, (ed. E. L. Bliss) (Harper and Brothers, New York, 1962), pp. 295-315.

CANNON, W. B., *Bodily Changes in Pain, Hunger, Fear and Rage* (Appleton-Century, New York, 1929).

CLARK, W. E. LE GROS, *The Antecedents of Man* (Edinburgh University Press, 1959).

COLBERT, E. H., *Evolution of the Vertebrates* (Wiley, New York, 1955).

COMFORT, A., *Nature and Human Nature* (Weidenfeld and Nicolson, 1966).

COSS, R. G., *Mood Provoking Visual Stimuli* (University of California, 1965).

DART, R. A. and D. CRAIG, *Advances with the Missing Link* (Hamish Hamilton, 1959).

EIMERL, S. and I. DEVORE, *The Primates* (Time Life, New York, 1965).

FORD, C. S. and F. A. BEACH, *Patterns of Sexual Behaviour* (Eyre and Spottiswoode, 1952).

FREMLIN, J. H., 'How many people can the world support?' *New Scientist* 24 (1965), pp. 285-7.

GOULD, G. M. and W. L. PYLE, *Anomalies and Curiosities of Medicine* (Saunders, Philadelphia, 1896).

GUGGISBERG, C. A. W., *Simba. The Life of the Lion* (Bailey Bros. and Swinfen, 1961).

GUNTHER, M., 'Instinct and the nursing couple'. *Lancet* (1955), pp. 575-8.

HARDY, A. C., 'Was man more aquatic in the past?' *New Scientist* 7 (1960), pp. 642-5.

HARLOW, H. F., 'The nature of love'. *Amer. Psychol.* 13 (1958), pp. 673-85.

HARRISON, G. A., J. S. WEINER, J. M. TANNER and N. A. BARNICOTT, *Human Biology* (Oxford University Press, 1964).

HAYES, C., *The Ape in our House* (Gollancz, 1952).

HOOTON, E. A., *Up from the Ape* (Macmillan, New York, 1947).

HOWELLS, W., *Mankind in the Making* (Secker and Warburg, 1960).

HUTT, C. and M. J. VAIZEY, 'Differential effects of group density on social behaviour'. *Nature* 209 (1966), pp. 1371-2.

KELLOGG, R., *What Children Scribble and Why* (Author's edition, San Francisco, 1955).

KINSEY, A. C., W. B. POMEROY and C. E. MARTIN, *Sexual Behaviour in the Human Male* (Saunders, Philadelphia, 1948).

KINSEY, A. C., W. B. POMEROY, C. E. MARTIN and P. H. GEBHARD, *Sexual Behaviour in the Human Female* (Saunders, Philadelphia, 1953).

KLEIMAN, D., 'Scent marking in the Canidae'. *Symp. Zool. Soc.* 18 (1966), pp. 167-77.

KLEITMAN, N., *Sleep and Wakefulness* (Chicago University Press, 1963).

KRUUK, H., 'Clan-system and feeding habits of Spotted Hyenas'. *Nature* 209 (1966), pp. 1257-8.

LEYHAUSEN, P., *Verhaltensstudien an Katzen* (Paul Parey, Berlin, 1956).

LIPSITT, L., 'Learning processes of human newborns'. *Merril-Palmer Quart. Behav. Devel.* 12 (1966), pp. 45-71.

LORENZ, K., *King Solomon's Ring* (Methuen, 1952).

LORENZ, K., *Man Meets Dog* (Methuen, 1954).

MARKS, I. M. and M. G. GELDER, 'Different onset ages in varieties of phobias'. *Amer. J. Psychiat.* (July 1966).

MASTERS, W. H. and V. E. JOHNSON, *Human Sexual Response* (Churchill, 1966).

MILES, W. R., 'Chimpanzee behaviour: removal of foreign body from companion's eye'. *Proc. Nat. Acad. Sci.* 49 (1963), pp. 840-3.

MONICREFF, R. W., 'Changes in olfactory preferences with age'. *Rev. Laryngol.* (1965), pp. 895-904.

MONTAGNA, W., *The Structure and Function of Skin* (Academic Press, London, 1956).

MONTAGU, M. F. A., *An Introduction to Physical Anthropology* (Thomas, Springfield, 1945).

MORRIS, D., 'The causation of pseudofemale and pseudomale behaviour'. *Behaviour* 8 (1955), pp. 46-56.

MORRIS, D., 'The function and causation of courtship ceremonies'. Fondation Singer Polignac Colloque Internat. sur L'Instinct, June 1954 (1956), pp. 261-86.

MORRIS, D., 'The feather postures of birds and the problem of the origin of social signals'. *Behaviour* 9 (1956), pp. 75-113.

MORRIS, D., '"Typical Intensity" and its relation to the problem of ritualization'. *Behaviour* 11 (1957), pp. 1-12.

MORRIS, D., *The Biology of Art* (Methuen, 1962).

MORRIS, D., 'The response of animals to a restricted environment'. *Symp. Zool. Soc. Lond.* 13 (1964), pp. 99-118.

MORRIS, D., *The Mammals: a Guide to the Living Species* (Hodder and Stoughton, 1965).

MORRIS, D., 'The rigidification of behaviour'. *Phil. Trans. Roy. Soc. London*, B. 251 (1966), pp. 327-30.

MORRIS, D. (editor), *Primate Ethology* (Weidenfeld and Nicolson, 1967).

MORRIS, R. and D. MORRIS, *Men and Snakes* (Hutchinson, 1965).

MORRIS, R. and D. MORRIS, *Men and Apes* (Hutchinson, 1966).

MORRIS, R. and D. MORRIS, *Men and Pandas* (Hutchinson, 1966).

MOULTON, D. G., E. H. ASHTON and J. T. EAYRS, 'Studies in olfactory acuity. 4. Relative detectability of n-Aliphatic acids by dogs'. *Anim. Behav.* 8 (1960), pp. 117-28.

NAPIER, J. and P. NAPIER, *Primate Biology* (Academic Press, 1967).

Neuhaus, W., 'Über die Riechschärfe der Hunden für Fettsäuren'. *Z. vergl. Physiol.* 35 (1953), pp. 527-52.

Oakley, K. P., *Man the Toolmaker*. Brit. Mus. (Nat. Hist.), 1961.

Read, C., *The Origin of Man* (Cambridge University Press, 1925).

Romer, A. S., *The Vertebrate Story* (Chicago University Press, 1958).

Russell, C. and W. M. S. Russell, *Human Behaviour* (André Deutsch, 1961).

Salk, L., 'Thoughts on the concept of imprinting and its place in early human development'. *Canad. Psychiat. Assoc. J.* 11 (1966), pp. 295-305.

Schaller, G., *The Mountain Gorilla* (Chicago University Press, 1963).

Shirley, M. M., 'The first two years, a study of twenty-five babies'. Vol. 2, *Intellectual development. Inst. Child Welf. Mongr.*, Serial No. 8 (University of Minnesota Press, Minneapolis, 1933).

Smith, M. E., 'An investigation of the development of the sentence and the extent of the vocabulary in young children'. *Univ. Iowa Stud. Child. Welf.* 3, No. 5 (1926).

Sparks, J., 'Social grooming in animals'. *New Scientist* 19 (1963), pp. 235-7.

Southwick, C. H. (editor), *Primate Social Behaviour* (van Nostrand, Princeton, 1963).

Tax, S. (editor), *The Evolution of Man* (Chicago University Press, 1960).

Tiger, L., Research report: Patterns of male association. *Current Anthropology* (vol. VIII, No. 3, June 1967).

Tinbergen, N., *The Study of Instinct* (Oxford University Press, 1951).

Van Hooff, J., 'Facial expressions in higher primates'. *Symp. Zool. Soc. Lond.* 8 (1962), pp. 97-125.

Washburn, S. L. (editor), *Social Life of Early Man* (Methuen, 1962).

Washburn, S. L. (editor), *Classification and Human Evolution* (Methuen, 1964).

Wickler, W., 'Die biologische Bedeutung auffallend farbiger, nackter Hautstellen und innerartliche

Mimikry der Primaten'. *Die Naturwissenschaften* 50 (13) (1963), pp. 481-2.

WICKLER, W., Socio-sexual signals and their intra-specific imitation among primates. In *Primate Ethology*, (ed. D. Morris) (Weidenfeld and Nicolson, 1967), pp. 68-147.

WYBURN, G. M., R. W. PICKFORD and R. J. HIRST, *Human Senses and Perception* (Oliver and Boyd, 1964).

YERKES, R. M. and A. W. YERKES, *The Great Apes* (Yale University Press, 1929).

YOUNG, P. and E. A. GOLDMAN, *The Wolves of North America* (Constable, 1944).

ZEUNER, F. E., *A History of Domesticated Animals* (Hutchinson, 1963).

ZUCKERMAN, S., *The Social Life of Monkeys and Apes* (Kegan Paul, 1932).

A selection of Bestsellers from Mayflower Books

Novels

EMMANUELLE	Emmanuelle Arsan	60p	☐
THE FURTHER EXPERIENCES OF			
EMMANUELLE	Emmanuelle Arsan	80p	☐
OIL	Jonathan Black	75p	☐
THE WORLD RAPERS	Jonathan Black	75p	☐
THE FOOTBALLER	Derek Dougan	75p	☐
PIPER'S LEAVE	Alexander Fullerton	60p	☐
OTHER MEN'S WIVES	Alexander Fullerton	50p	☐
BURY THE PAST	Alexander Fullerton	50p	☐
THE ESCAPISTS	Alexander Fullerton	50p	☐
THE PUBLISHER	Alexander Fullerton	50p	☐
STORE	Alexander Fullerton	40p	☐
CHIEF EXECUTIVE	Alexander Fullerton	50p	☐
, A SAILOR	Morgen Holm	60p	☐
, A PROSTITUTE	Nina Holm	35p	☐
, A WOMAN	Siv Holm	35p	☐
, SUSANNE	Susanne Holm	40p	☐
, A TEENAGER	Tine Holm	40p	☐
KOPTIC COURT	Herbert Kastle	75p	☐
THE WORLD THEY WANTED	Herbert Kastle	75p	☐
LITTLE LOVE	Herbert Kastle	50p	☐
MILLIONAIRES	Herbert Kastle	75p	☐
MIAMI GOLDEN BOY	Herbert Kastle	60p	☐
THE MOVIE MAKER	Herbert Kastle	95p	☐
THE STORY OF SAN MICHELE	Axel Munthe	75p	☐
AMANDA IN SPAIN	George Revelli	50p	☐
AMANDA'S CASTLE	George Revelli	35p	☐
RESORT TO WAR	George Revelli	35p	☐
COMMANDER AMANDA NIGHTINGALE			
	George Revelli	35p	☐
DOCTOR, NO!	William Rice	50p	☐
DOCTOR, DON'T!	William Rice	50p	☐
AN INTERRUPTED FRIENDSHIP	E. L. Voynich	50p	☐
THE GADFLY	E. L. Voynich	40p	☐
THE COAST OF FEAR	Leslie Waller	60p	☐
NUMBER ONE	Leslie Waller	60p	☐
A CHANGE IN THE WIND	Leslie Waller	40p	☐
THE AMERICAN	Leslie Waller	60p	☐

Novels

THE FAMILY	Leslie Waller	90p ☐
THE BANKER	Leslie Waller	£1.00 ☐
STRAW DOGS	Gordon Williams	60p ☐
THE CAMP	Gordon Williams	35p ☐
THE UPPER PLEASURE GARDEN		
	Gordon Williams	40p ☐
FROM SCENES LIKE THESE	Gordon Williams	30p ☐
RAMBLING ROSE	Calder Willingham	50p ☐
END AS A MAN	Calder Willingham	50p ☐
GERALDINE BRADSHAW	Calder Willingham	40p ☐
ETERNAL FIRE	Calder Willingham	60p ☐
PROVIDENCE ISLAND	Calder Willingham	75p ☐
REACH TO THE STARS	Calder Willingham	35p ☐
TO EAT A PEACH	Calder Willingham	40p ☐
WANDERERS EASTWARD, WANDERERS WEST		
(Vol 1)	Kathleen Winsor	95p ☐
WANDERERS EASTWARD, WANDERERS WEST		
(Vol 2)	Kathleen Winsor	95p ☐

All these books are available at your local bookshop or newsagent, or can be ordered direct from the publisher. Just tick the titles you want and fill in the form below.

Name ....

Address ....

••   ••••••••••••••••••••••••••

Write to Mayflower Cash Sales, PO Box 11, Falmouth, Cornwall TR10 9EN

Please enclose remittance to the value of the cover price plus:

UK: 18p for the first book plus 8p per copy for each additional book ordered to a maximum charge of 66p

BFPO and EIRE: 18p for the first book plus 8p per copy for the next 6 books, thereafter 3p per book

OVERSEAS: 20p for first book and 10p for each additional book

Granada Publishing reserve the right to show new retail prices on covers, which may differ from those previously advertised in the text or elsewhere.